✳ At a Glance

Essays

✳ At a Glance

Essays

FOURTH EDITION

Lee Brandon
Mt. San Antonio College

Houghton Mifflin Company   *Boston   New York*

To Sharon

Executive Publisher: Patricia A. Coryell
Editor in Chief: Carrie Brandon
Sponsoring Editor: Joann Kozyrev
Senior Marketing Manager: Tom Ziolkowski
Associate Project Editor: Deborah Thomashow
Cover Design Director: Tony Saizon
Senior Composition Buyer: Chuck Dutton
New Title Project Manager: Susan Peltier
Editorial Assistant: Daisuke Yasutake
Marketing Assistant: Bettina Chiu

Cover image: © Judith Gosse/Getty Images

Acknowledgments and copyrights appear on page 250, which constitutes
an extension of the copyright page.

Printed in the U.S.A.

Library of Congress Control Number: 2007940569

ISBN-10: 0-618-95763-4
ISBN-13: 978-0-618-95763-7

23456789-EB-12 11 10 09 08

✳ Contents

Components of Your Essay   177
Kinds of Evidence   177

Practicing Patterns of Argument   178
Examining Essays of Argument   179

Student Writer   179

"Teaching Our Kids to Shoot 'Em Up"   *Tina Sergio*   179

Professional Writer   182

"Graffiti: Taking a Closer Look"   *Christopher Grant*   182

Topics for Essays of Argument   188

Reading-Related and Text-Based Topics   188
Cross-Curricular Topics   189
Career-Related Topics   189
General Topics   189

Writer's Guidelines at a Glance: Argument   190

13   The Research Paper   191

The Research Paper Defined   191
Ten Steps to Writing a Research Paper   191

1. Select a Topic   191
2. Find Sources   193
3. List Sources   195
4. Take Notes   204
5. Refine Your Thesis and Outline   205
6. Write Your First Draft   205
7. Revise Your First Draft   210
8. Prepare Your Works Cited Page   210
9. Write Your Final Draft   210
10. Submit Required Materials   210

Student Example   212

"Zoos—An Endangered Species?"   *Michael Chung*   212

Writer's Guidelines at a Glance: The Research Paper   222

14   Handbook   223

Subjects and Verbs   223
Kinds of Sentences   224
Sentence Problems   226

✳ Preface

At a Glance: Essays is the third-level book in the *At a Glance* series. Along with *At a Glance: Sentences, At a Glance: Paragraphs,* and *At a Glance: Reader,* it meets the current need for succinct, comprehensive, and up-to-date textbooks that students can afford. All four books provide basic instruction, exercises, and writing assignments at the designated level, as well as support material for instructors. *At a Glance: Sentences* and *At a Glance: Paragraphs* include a transition to the next level of writing, while *At a Glance: Paragraphs, At a Glance: Essays,* and *At a Glance: Reader* each ends with a handbook, to which students can refer for help with sentence-level issues or for problems with mechanics. *At a Glance: Reader* presents brief writing instruction and thirty sources for reading-related and text-based writing. Each book in the *At a Glance* series can be used alone, with one of the other *At a Glance* books, or with another textbook. Two or more *At a Glance* books can be shrink-wrapped and delivered at a discount.

✳ Comprehensive Coverage

Chapter 1, Reading for Writing, guides students in writing about what they read, with emphasis on the summary, the reaction, and the two-part response. Chapters 2–4 cover the writing process: prewriting techniques, first-draft writing, revising, and editing. Each phase is illustrated with student examples. Chapters 5–12 present eight patterns of essay writing, with a chapter devoted to each: descriptive narration, exemplification, analysis by division, process analysis, cause and effect, comparison and contrast, definition, and argument.

Chapter 13, The Research Paper, includes forms of documentation as well as a discussion of libraries, online searching, plagiarism, and other research-related topics. *At a Glance: Essays* concludes with Chapter 14, a handbook that addresses sentence-level issues (subjects and verbs, fragments, coordination and subordination, sentence variety, and so on); specific verb, pronoun, omission, and modifier problems; and punctuation and capitalization.

✳ Instructional Approach

The instruction in *At a Glance: Essays* is concise and direct, using thought-provoking examples of essays by student and professional writers and a variety of exercises. Each of Chapters 5 through 12 follows the same sequence: writing strategies for a particular essay pattern, an exercise that gives students practice in organizing the pattern, an annotated student example, a professional example with critical thinking questions, topic suggestions (text-based and reading related, cross-curricular, career-related, and general) for writing such essays, and a summary of guidelines specific to the pattern.

This edition features

- NEW instruction on the summary, reaction, and two-part response as text-based writing
- a Writing Process Worksheet, designed to provide guidance for students and save time and effort for instructors
- a streamlined Self-Evaluation Chart to help students track their needs and goals and promote self-reliance
- a section on paragraphs for introduction, support, and conclusion
- sixteen new (75 percent) readings selections
- a research paper unit organized around the ten steps of the writing process
- lists of text-based and reading-related, cross-curricular, career related, and general topics in Chapters 5–12
- NEW examples of documented student essays
- an expanded handbook section, including units on diction, sentence variety, and omissions

✳ Support Material for Instructors

NEW! HM WriteSPACE™ encompasses the interactive online products and services integrated with Houghton Mifflin (Developmental Writing and Composition) textbook programs. Students and instructors can access HM WriteSPACE™ content through text-specific student and instructor websites, via Eduspace®, Houghton Mifflin's online Course Management System, and through additional course management systems including BlackBoard®/WebCT®. The following descriptions provide further information regarding the online services that are available specifically with the *At a Glance* series.

- **Instructor Website for *At a Glance.*** The Instructor Website provides helpful resources such as sample syllabi, teaching tips, reproducible quizzes, PowerPoint slides, and Answer Keys. Access to the website can be found by visiting college .hmco.com/pic/brandonAGE4e
- **Student Website for *At a Glance.*** The Student Website provides helpful resources such as sentence writing exercises, a brief illustrated guide to documented papers, a printable Writing Process Worksheet, tips on resumes and letters of application, and additional reading selections. Access to the website can be found by visiting college.hmco.com/pic/brandon AGE4e.
- **HM WriteSPACE™ with Eduspace® Online Writing Program.** Eduspace®, Houghton Mifflin's Course Management System, offers instructors a flexible, interactive online platform to communicate with students, organize material, evaluate student work, and track results in a powerful gradebook. In addition to HM WriteSPACE™ resources, students and instructors using Eduspace® benefit from Course Management, Tools Practice Exercises, Online Homework, HM Assess, Safe Assignment, and an Online Handbook.

✳ Acknowledgments

I am profoundly indebted to the following instructors who have reviewed this textbook: Connie A. Gramza, Erie Community College; Janice Hart, Central New Mexico Community College; Charlotte Laughlin, McLennan Community College; and Buzz R. Pounds, Lewis University. Thanks also to members of the English Department at Mt. San Antonio College, with special recognition to the Basic Courses Review Committee.

I deeply appreciate the work of Nancy Benjamin of Books By Design; freelance editor Mary Dalton Hoffman; and my colleagues at Houghton Mifflin: Joann Kozyrev, Judith Fifer, Tom Ziolkowski, Daisuke Yasutake, Bettina Chiu, and Deborah Thomashow.

I am especially grateful to my family of wife, children and their spouses, and grandchildren for their cheerful, inspiring support: Sharon, Kelly, Erin, Kathy, Michael, Shane, Lauren, Jarrett, and Matthew.

Lee Brandon

❉ Student Overview

This book is designed to help you write better essays and research papers. Chapter 1 introduces you to writing about what you read. Chapter 2 defines the essay and discusses what you need to know and do to write effective essays. Chapters 3 and 4 focus on the writing process itself—how to get started and how to develop, revise, and edit your working drafts. Every stage is illustrated by the work of one student, whom we follow through the entire process.

Each of Chapters 5 through 12 describes a different pattern for developing an essay. For example, Chapter 5 is about writing an essay by using both description and storytelling techniques, and Chapter 12 is about writing an essay of argument. Each of Chapters 5 through 12 includes one essay written by a student and one written by a professional writer. In every chapter, questions and exercises help you put into practice what you have learned.

Chapter 13 explains and illustrates the ten steps to writing the research paper and describes the special considerations that kind of essay involves. The book ends with Chapter 14, a handbook, to which you can refer whenever you needed assistance in grammar, usage, punctuation, and capitalization.

Following are some strategies to help you make the best use of this book and to jump-start the improvement in your writing skills.

1. **Be active and systematic in learning.** Take advantage of your instructor's expertise by being an active participant in class—one who takes notes, asks questions, and contributes to discussion. Become dedicated to systematic learning: determine your needs, decide what to do, and do it. Make learning a part of your everyday thinking and behavior.
2. **Read widely.** Samuel Johnson, a great English scholar, once said he didn't want to read anything by people who had written more than they had read. William Faulkner, a Nobel Prize winner in literature, said, "Read, read, read. Read everything—trash, classics, good and bad, and see how writers do it." Read to learn technique, to acquire ideas, to be stimulated to write. Especially

read to satisfy your curiosity and receive pleasure. If reading is a main component of your course, approach it as systematically as you do writing. Text-based writing will offer you opportunities to polish your critical-thinking skills as you compose responses to what you read, much as you do in classes across the curriculum.

3. **Keep a journal.** Keeping a journal may not be required in your particular class, but whether required or not, jotting down your observations in a notebook is a good idea. Here are some ideas for daily, or almost daily, journal writing:

- Summarize, evaluate, or react to reading assignments.
- Summarize, evaluate, or react to what you see on television and in movies, and to what you read in newspapers and magazines.
- Describe and narrate situations or events you experience.
- Write about career-related matters you encounter in other courses or on the job.

Your journal entries may read like an intellectual diary, a record of what you are thinking about at certain times. Because your entries are not structured writing assignments, organization and editing are not important. Mainly, keeping a journal will help you to understand reading material better, to develop more language skills, and to think more clearly—as well as to become more confident and write more easily so that writing becomes a comfortable everyday activity. Your entries may also provide subject material for longer, more carefully crafted pieces. It is important to get into the habit of writing something each day.

4. **Evaluate your writing skills.** Use the Self-Evaluation Chart inside the front cover of this book to list areas you need to work on. You can add to your lists throughout the entire term. Drawing on your instructor's comments, make notes on matters such as the organization, development, and content of your essays; spelling, vocabulary, and diction; and so on. Use the chart for self-motivated study assignments and as a checklist in all stages of writing. As you master each problem area, you can check it off or cross it out.

Here is a partially filled out Self-Evaluation Chart, followed by some guidelines for filling out your own.

Self-Evaluation Chart

Organization/ Development/ Content	Spelling/ Vocabulary/ Diction	Grammar/ Sentence Structure	Punctuation/ Capitalization
Avoid top-heavy intro-ductions 26–29 Use specific examples 89 Repeat key words such as *causes* and *effects* 59	all right separate sophomore avoid "into" as "into rap" 57	Vary sentence beginnings 61–62 Watch for pronoun antecedent problems, such as "a person . . . they" 239 RO-CS—*Then* isn't a conjunc-tion 62	comma after long introductory modifier 243 colon to intro-duce list 246 cap beginning for words replacing names, such as, "I told Mother," but "I told my mother" 249

- *Organization/Development/Content.* Note your instructor's suggestions for all aspects of planning your essays and supporting your ideas.
- *Spelling/Vocabulary/Diction.* List words marked as incorrectly spelled on your assignments. Master the words on your list and add new words as you accumulate assignments. List suggestions made by your instructor about word choice (such as avoiding slang, clichés, and vague terms). Also include new, useful words you encounter in this class and others; add the words here, with simple definitions. Use another page if you need more space.
- *Grammar/Sentence Structure.* List any grammar points you need to remember or any sentence problems, such as frag-ments, comma splices, and run-ons. If you tend to begin sen-tences in the same way or to choose the same patterns, use your chart to remind yourself to vary your sentence beginnings and patterns.
- *Punctuation/Capitalization.* List any problems you encounter with punctuation and capitalization. Because the items in this column may be covered in Chapter 14, you can often use both rule numbers and page numbers for the references here.

5. **Take full advantage of the** *At a Glance* **Student Website and other technology.** Using a computer will enable you to write, revise, and edit more swiftly as you move, alter, check, and delete material with a few keystrokes. The Student Website offers additional exercises and instruction. Many colleges have writing labs with good instruction and facilities for networking and researching complicated topics. The Internet, used wisely, can provide resource material for compositions.

6. **Use the Writing Process Worksheet.** Record details about each of your assignments, such as the due date, topic, length, and form. The worksheet will also remind you of the stages of the writing process: explore, organize, and write. A blank Writing Process Worksheet for you to enlarge and photocopy for assignments appears on page xxi, and a printable copy is on your Student Website.

7. **Be positive.** All the elements you record in your Self-Evaluation Chart are probably covered in *At a Glance: Essays.* The table of contents, the index, and the Correction Chart on the inside back cover of the book will direct you to the additional instruction you decide you need. Soon, seeing what you have mastered and checked off your list will give you a sense of accomplishment.

Finally, don't compare yourself with others. Compare yourself with yourself and, as you make progress, consider yourself what you are—a student on the path toward effective writing, a student on the path toward success.

Writing Process Worksheet

Title_____

Name_____ Due Date _____

Assignment   In the space below, write whatever you need to know about your assignment, including information about the topic, audience, pattern of writing, length, whether to include a rough draft or revised drafts, and whether your paper must be typed.

Stage One   **Explore**   Freewrite, brainstorm (list), cluster, or take notes as directed by your instructor. Use the back of this page or separate paper, if you need more space.

Stage Two   **Organize**   Write a topic sentence or thesis; label the subject and treatment parts.

Write an outline or a structured list. For text-based writing, include quotations and references and page numbers.

Stage Three   **Write**   On separate paper, write and then revise your paragraph or essay as many times as necessary for **c**oherence, **l**anguage (usage, tone, and diction), **u**nity, **e**mphasis, **s**upport, and **s**entences (**CLUESS**). Read your work aloud to hear and correct any grammatical errors or awkward-sounding sentences.

Edit any problems in fundamentals, such as **c**apitalization, **o**missions, **p**unctuation, and **s**pelling (**COPS**).

xxi

✳ At a Glance
Essays

✴ 1

Reading for Writing

✴ Text-Based and Reading-Related Writing

Whether on campus or at the workplace, your skill in identifying main ideas and their support through reading and then commenting on them in writing will serve you well. The writing you will be introduced to in this chapter is commonly called text-based writing. A similar form is reading-related writing, which uses sources for ideas and pattern but has less critical focus on content. Chapters 5–12 include topics in text-based and reading-related writing along with general, cross-curricular, and career-related writing.

Text-based writing includes

- reading effectively (which may include underlining and annotating).
- writing a **summary** (main ideas in your own words).
- writing a **reaction** (usually a statement of how the reading relates specifically to you, your experiences, and your attitudes but also can be a critique of content and logic).
- writing a **two-part response** (both a summary and a reaction, although they are separate).
- documenting (giving credit to sources you use).

All of these kinds of text-based writing

- originate as a response to something you have read.
- indicate, to some degree, content from that piece.
- demonstrate your knowledge of that piece.

Underlining and annotating will give you practice in reading analytically and in recording the main ideas and their support in a clear, direct manner.

Underlining

Imagine you are reading a chapter of several pages and you decide to underline and write in the margins. Immediately, the underlining

1

takes you out of the passive, television-watching frame of mind. You are involved. You are participating. It is now necessary for you to discriminate, to distinguish more important from less important ideas. Perhaps you have thought of underlining as a method designed only to help you with reviewing. That is, when you study the material the next time, you will not have to reread all of it; instead, you can review only the most important, underlined parts. However, even while you are underlining, you are benefiting from an imposed concentration because this procedure forces you to think, to focus. Consider the following guidelines for underlining:

1. Underline the main ideas in paragraphs. The most important statement, the topic sentence, is likely to be at the beginning of the paragraph.
2. Underline the support for those main ideas.
3. Underline answers to questions that you bring to the reading assignment. These questions may have come from the end of the chapter, from subheadings that you turn into questions, or from your independent concerns about the topic.
4. Underline only the key words. You would seldom underline all the words in a sentence and almost never a whole paragraph.

Does that fit your approach to underlining? Possibly not. Most students, in their enthusiasm to do a good job, overdo underlining.

The trick is to figure out what to underline. You would seldom underline more than about 30 percent of a passage, although the amount would depend on your purpose and the nature of the material. Following the preceding four suggestions will be useful. Learning more about the principles of sentence, paragraph, and essay organization in the following chapters will also be helpful.

Annotating

Annotating, writing notes in the margins, is a practice related to underlining. You can do it independently, although it usually appears in conjunction with underlining to record your understanding and to extend your involvement in your reading.

Writing in the margins represents intense involvement because it turns a reader into a writer. If you read material and write something in the margin as a reaction to it, then in a way you have had a conversation with the author. The author has made a statement and you have responded. In fact, you may have added something to the text; therefore, for your purposes, you have become a co-author or collaborator. The comments you make in the margin are of your own choosing according to your interests and the purpose you bring to the reading assignment. Your response in the margin may merely echo the author's ideas, may question them critically, may relate them to something else, or may add to them.

The comments and marks on the following essay will help you understand the connection between writing and reading. Both techniques—underlining to indicate main and supporting ideas and annotating to indicate their importance and relevance to the task at hand—will enhance thinking, reading, and writing.

Total Institutions

Seymour Feshbach and Bernard Weiner

Total institution encompasses individual (thesis)	1	A <u>total institution</u> completely <u>encompasses</u> the <u>individual</u>, forming a barrier to the types of social intercourse that occur outside such a setting. Monasteries, jails, homes for the aged, boarding schools, and military academies are a few examples of total institutions.
1. Individual activities in same setting	2	<u>Total institutions</u> have certain <u>common characteristics</u>. <u>First</u>, the <u>individuals</u> in such environments must <u>sleep</u>, <u>play</u>, and <u>work</u> within the <u>same setting</u>. These are generally segmented spheres of activity in the lives of most individuals, but within a total institution one sphere of activity overlaps
2. All life within group		with others. <u>Second, each phase of life</u> takes place in the <u>company</u> of a <u>large group</u> of others. Frequently, sleeping is done in a barracks, food is served in a cafeteria, and so on. In such activities everyone is treated alike and must perform certain
3. Activities tightly scheduled		essential tasks. <u>Third, activities</u> in an institution are <u>tightly scheduled</u> according to a <u>master plan</u>, with set times to rise, to eat, to exercise, and to sleep. These institutional characteristics result in a <u>bureaucratic society</u>, which requires the hiring of other people for surveillance. What often results is a split in the groups within an institution into a large, managed group (inmates) and a small
Managed groups and staff at distance		supervisory staff. There tends to be <u>great social distance between</u> the <u>groups</u>, who <u>perceive each other according to stereotypes</u> and <u>have</u> severely <u>restricted communications</u>.

Two worlds—	3	The world of the inmate differs greatly from
inside and		the outside world. When one enters a total institu-
outside		tion, all previous roles, such as father or husband,

The world of the inmate differs greatly from the outside world. When one enters a total institution, all previous roles, such as father or husband, are disrupted. The individual is further depersonalized by the issuance of a uniform, confiscation of belongings, and gathering of personal information, as well as by more subtle touches like doorless toilets, record keeping, and bedchecks. The effects of an institutional setting are so all-encompassing that one can meaningfully speak of an "institutional personality: a persistent manner of behaving compliantly and without emotional involvement.

Personality altered

4   Of course, there are individual differences in adaptation to the situation. They can be as extreme as psychosis, childlike regression, and depression or as mild as resigned compliance. Most individuals do adjust and build up a system of satisfactions, such as close friendships and cliques.

Becomes psychotic, childlike, or depressive

5   But because of these bonds and the fact that the habits needed to function in the outside world have been lost, inmates face great problems upon leaving an institution. A shift from the top of a small society to the bottom of a larger one may be further demoralizing.

Individuals adjust but have trouble later on street

Exercise 1   Underlining and Annotating

Underline and annotate this passage.

Effective E-Mail Practices

Use short lines and short paragraphs. A short line length (perhaps 50 to 60 characters) is much easier to read than the 80-character line of most text editors. Similarly, short paragraphs (especially the first and last paragraph) are more inviting to read. Avoid formatting a long message as one solid paragraph.

Don't shout. Use all-capital letters only for emphasis or to substitute for italicized text (such as book titles). Do NOT type your entire message in all capitals: It is a text-based form of *shouting* at your reader and is considered rude (not to mention more difficult to read).

Proofread your message before sending it. Do not let the speed and convenience of e-mail lull you into being careless. While an occasional typo or other surface error will probably be overlooked by the reader, excessive errors or sloppy language creates an unprofessional image of the sender.

Append previous messages appropriately. Most e-mail systems allow you to append the original message to your reply. Use this feature judiciously. Occasionally, it may be helpful for the reader to see his or her entire message replayed. More often, however, you can save the reader time by establishing the context of the original message in your reply. If necessary, quote pertinent parts of the original message. If the entire original message is needed, treat it as an appendix and insert it at the *end* of your reply—not at the beginning.

Use a direct style of writing and think twice; write once. Put your major idea in the first sentence or two. If the message is so sensitive or emotionally laden that a more indirect organization would be appropriate, you should reconsider whether e-mail is the most effective medium for the message. Because it is so easy to respond immediately to a message, you might be tempted to let your emotions take over. Such behavior is called "flaming" and should be avoided. Always assume the message you send will never be destroyed but will be saved permanently in somebody's computer file.

Do not neglect your greeting and closing. Downplay the seeming impersonality of computerized mail by starting your message with a friendly salutation, such as "Hi, Amos" or "Dear Mr. Fisher."

An effective closing is equally important. Some e-mail programs identify only the e-mail address (for example, "705@compuserve .com") in the message header they transmit. Do not take a chance that your reader will not recognize you. Include your name, e-mail address, and any other appropriate identifying information at the end of your message.

—Adapted from Scot Ober, *Contemporary Business Communication*

✳ Types of Writing

Personal Narrative

Some of the student and professional reading selections in this book will be of a personal nature. Often it will be in a narrative (story) form and may include opinion. Mastering this kind of personal writing is important because you have accumulated many valuable and interesting experiences.

Analytical and Text-Based Writing

Many more college writing tasks, however, will require you to evaluate and reflect on ideas. These ideas may come from what you have learned collectively. They may also come from reading. Often you will be expected to read, to think, and to write critically. These reading-related writing assignments will direct you to respond in the principal forms of text-based writing: the summary and the reaction (evaluation, analysis, interpretation), which may be combined for a two-part response to distinguish each part. All three are forms of text-based writing. Think of text-based writing as responding in detail with direct references and quotations to what you have read and giving credit to the author(s) of that material. Such a process of reading and writing demonstrates you understanding of your source(s) and is the essence of critical thinking.

Writing a Summary

A **summary** is a rewritten, shortened version of a piece of writing in which you use your own wording to express the main ideas. Learning to summarize effectively will help you in many ways. Summary writing reinforces comprehension skills in reading. It requires you to discriminate among the ideas in the target reading passage. Summaries are usually written in the form of a well-designed paragraph or set of paragraphs. Frequently, they are used in collecting material for research papers and in writing conclusions to essays.

The following rules will guide you in writing effective summaries.

1. Cite the author and title of the text.
2. Reduce the length of the original by about two-thirds, although the exact reduction will vary, depending on the content of the original.
3. Concentrate on the main ideas and include details only infrequently.
4. Change the original wording without changing the idea.
5. Do not evaluate the content or give an opinion in any way (even if you see an error in logic or fact).
6. Do not add ideas (even if you have an abundance of related information).
7. Do not include any personal comments (that is, do not use *I*, referring to self).

8. Use quotations only infrequently. (If you do use quotations, however, enclose them in quotation marks.)
9. Use some author tags ("says York," "according to York," or "the author explains") to remind the reader(s) that you are summarizing the material of another author.

Exercise 2 | Evaluating a Summary

Apply the rules of summary writing to the following summary of "Total Institutions," p. 3. Mark the instances of poor summary writing by using rule numbers from the preceding list.

Total Institutions

A total institution completely encompasses the individual. Total institutions have certain common characteristics. Institutions provide the setting for all rest, recreation, and labor. Residents function only within the group. And residents are directed by a highly organized schedule, which, I think, is what they need or they wouldn't be there. There residents are depersonalized by being required to wear a uniform, abandon personal items, and give up privacy. Some adapt in a negative way by developing psychological problems, but most adapt in a positive way by forming relationships with other residents. Several popular movies, such as *The Shawshank Redemption,* show how prison society works, to use one example. Once outside the total institution, individuals must deal with the problem of relearning old coping habits. They must also withstand the shock of going from the top of a small society to the bottom of a larger one. Society needs these total institutions, especially the jails.

The following is an example of an effective summary.

A Summary of "Total Institutions"

Michael Balleau

In "Total Institutions," Seymour Feshbach and Bernard Weiner explain that a total institution encompasses the lives of its residents, who share three common traits: The residents must do everything in the same place, must do things together, and must do things according to the institution's schedule. The institution takes away the residents' roles they had in society, takes away their appearance by issuing uniforms, takes away their personal property by confiscation, and takes away their privacy by making life communal. The authors say that some residents adapt negatively by developing psychological problems, but most form relationships and new roles within the institution. Upon release, these residents must learn to function in the free world all over again, as they start at the bottom of society. This shift "may be further demoralizing."

Writing a Reaction

The reaction statement is another kind of text-based writing, one in which you incorporate your views. Some reactions require evaluation with a critical-thinking emphasis. Some focus on simple discussion of the content presented in the reading and include summary material. Others concentrate on the writer's experience as related to the content of the passage.

The following paragraph is student Tanya Morris's reaction statement to "Total Institutions." She could have expanded her ideas to write an essay. Her instructor did not require her to provide page-number locations of her references and quotations.

Institutions Always Win

Tanya Morris

The short essay "Total Institutions," by

Seymour Feshbach and Bernard Weiner, is a

study of conflicts in controlled
environments. The common characteristics of
such places are in personal combat with the
individual, in which the resident is stripped
of his or her choices and made to "sleep,
play, and work within the same setting." The
resident who tries to assert his or her
uniqueness is controlled by a master plan.
That plan is enforced by personnel who become
the masters of surveillance, set up social
barriers, and maintain control over their
underlings. The result is "a bureaucratic
society." Cut off from the free world, the
resident is in conflict with significant
matters of newness--clothes, facilities,
regulations, and roles. The authors explain
that almost always the institution wins,
sometimes converting the resident into a
disturbed person or an amiable robot among
other inmates. But at some point after that
conversion, the institutionalized person may
be returned to the free world. There a new
conflict arises for the inmate, who goes from
"the top of a small society to the bottom of
a larger one." The authors of this essay are
very clear in showing just how comprehensive
these institutions are in waging their war,
regardless of the motives, against
individuality. After all, they are "total."
As such, they should be, whenever possible,
avoided.

Writing a Two-Part Response

As you have seen, the reaction response includes a partial summary
or is written with the assumption that readers have read the original piece. However, your instructor may prefer that you separate each
form—for example, by presenting a clear, concise summary followed

by a reaction response. This format is especially useful for critical examination of a text or for problem-solving assignments because it requires you to understand and repeat another's views or experiences before responding. The two-part approach also helps you avoid the common problem of writing only a summary of the text when your instructor wants you to both summarize and evaluate or otherwise react. In writing a summary and a reaction it is a good idea to ask your instructor if you should separate your summary from your response.

Total Institutions: A Summary and a Reaction

Michael Balleau

Part I: Summary

In "Total Institutions," Seymour Feshbach
and Bernard Weiner explain that a total
institution encompasses the lives of its
residents, who share three common traits: The
residents must do everything in the same
place, must do things together, and must do
things according to the institution's
schedule. The institution takes away the
residents' roles they had in society, takes
away their appearance by issuing uniforms,
takes away their personal property by
confiscation, and takes away their privacy by
making life communal. The authors say that
some residents adapt negatively by developing
psychological problems, but most form
relationships and new roles within the
institution. Upon release, these residents

must learn to function in the free world all
over again as they start at the bottom of
society. This shift "may be further
demoralizing."

Part 2: Reaction [Page number documentation was not required.]

The basic ideas in "Total Institutions"
gave me an insight into the behavior of my
older cousin. Let's call him George. He spent
almost five years in prison for a white-
collar crime he committed at the bank where
he worked. Before George was incarcerated, he
was an individual, almost to the extreme of
being a rebel. When he got out, he was
clearly an institutionalized person.
Following the pattern of institutionalized
behavior laid out in "Total Institutions,"
George had become a group person without
knowing it. Many of "the habits needed to
function in the outside world [had] been
lost." Even at home after he returned, he had
to be around people. He wanted some of us to
be with him all the time, and he liked the
noise of a radio or television. When we went
out, he found it difficult to make decisions,
even in buying a simple item, such as a
shirt, or ordering food in a restaurant. Once
when he was driving, we were stopped by a

police officer because his car's taillight
was out, and George became transformed into
someone who was on automatic pilot in
answering questions. It was his
"institutional personality." Minutes later,
he seemed hostile and had bad, unwarranted
things to say about the officer. Altogether,
George did five years in prison, and it took
him about three more to adjust before he
seemed like sort of what he was before. He
was certainly never the same. As the authors
say, every person reacts differently to
"total institutions," and some institutions
are more extreme than others, but each one
has a profound effect on the resident's
individuality.

✳ Kinds of Support for Text-Based Writing

In your text-based writing assignments, you are likely to use three methods in developing your ideas: explanations, direct references to the reading selection, and quotations from the reading selection.

- Your explanations will often be expressed in patterns, such as causes and effects, comparison and contrast, definition, or exemplification. These forms are presented in depth in Chapters 5 through 12.
- Your references will point your reader(s) directly toward original ideas in sources. The more specific the references, the more helpful they will be to your readers.
- Your quotations will be words borrowed from sources and credited to those sources. You will use quotation marks around those words, which will appear as sentences or as partial sentences blended with your own words.

These concepts are important in all reading-related writing, but they are especially important in the text-based writing you will be doing in Chapters 5 through 12 of this textbook.

✳ Basic Documentation in Text-Based Writing

Borrowing words or ideas without giving credit to the originator is called **plagiarism** and is not acceptable scholarship, whether it is intentional or not. As you use sources from your textbook, your instructor will ask you to document the ideas of others formally or informally. Informally, you will credit a source by title or author's name. Formally, you will indicate the precise location of all the original ideas you have borrowed according to a system. (See pages 206–207, "Plagiarism," for more details.)

Citations

Documenting sources for papers based on written materials is systematic. Most English instructors use MLA (Modern Language Association) style, the system used in this chapter and explained in detail in Chapter 13, "The Research Paper." Mainly, you need to remember that when using material from a source, you must give enough information so that the reader will recognize it or be able to find it in its original context. Here are the most common principles of documentation that can be used for textbook or other restricted sources, whether it is quoted, paraphrased (restated), or summarized.

If you use the author's name in introducing a quotation, then usually give only the page number.

> EXAMPLE   Suzanne Britt says that "neat people are bums and clods at heart" (255).

If you use the author's name in introducing a borrowed idea, then usually give only the page number.

> EXAMPLE   Suzanne Britt believes that neat people are weak in character (255).

If you do not use the author's name to introduce a quotation or an idea, then usually give both the author's name and the page number:

> EXAMPLE   Music often helps Alzheimer's patients think more clearly (Weiss 112).

Works Cited

Work(s) Cited lists the sources used, meaning those that appear in citations, as shown in the previous section. Each kind of publication has its own order of parts and punctuation. You need not memorize them. They are given in detail in Chapter 13, on pages 191–222 and can be found on the Internet by keying in "MLA Form."

Here is an example of a Work Cited entry for a student writing. Other examples can be found at the end of the student works in this book and on pages 196–204. Note the punctuation between parts and the order of those parts: author's name (last, first), title of composition (quotation marks for a short work, italics for a long work), editor(s) of the anthology, name of the anthology, place of publication, publisher, date of publication, and pages on which the selection appears.

```
                        Work Cited
     Blaylock, Richard. "More Than the Classroom."
          Paragraphs and Essays with Integrated Readings.
          10th ed. Ed. Lee Brandon and Kelly Brandon. Boston:
          Houghton, 2008. 228.
```

✳ Documentation in Action

Your text-based paragraph or essay may include ideas from newspapers, magazines, or books. To make classwork simpler for you, most of the reading-related assignments in this book are based on selections included in this book. When you are writing about something you have read, just write as you usually would, but bring in ideas and quotations from that source. You may also want to refer to more than one source. You may even use ideas from other sources to contrast with your own. For example, you may say, "Unlike Fred M. Hechlinger in 'The First Step in Improving Sex Education: Remove the Hellfire' (351), I believe that public schools should not offer sex education." Do not feel that each point you make must be directly related to sources.

Student Documented Paragraph

Here is a student paragraph illustrating how to incorporate ideas and document them.

Sexist Men as Victims
Jackie Malone

Sexist men are victims of their own bias
against females. Because they cannot accept
women as full human beings, they themselves
are smaller in dimension. In Irwin Shaw's
"The Girls in Their Summer Dresses," Michael
looks at his wife, but he doesn't see a full
human being, he just sees a sexual object:
"what a pretty girl, what nice legs" (314).
Because he sees her and other women that way,
he cannot ever have the relationship with her
that she deserves and that he would find
fulfilling. Of course, thinking of women as
just soft and cuddly has its effects on men
in other ways. The man as father who thinks
that way may very well regard his own
daughter as one limited in her ranges of
activities and limited in her potential. He
may be one of those fathers who immediately
stereotype their daughters as headed for a
"life of the affections," not like a son's,
"earning a living" (Lurie 249).
Unfortunately, these men cannot accept
females as their equals in any important
respect, and, in doing so, they deprive
themselves, as well as others.

Works Cited

Lurie, Alison. "Pink Kittens and Blue
    Spaceships." Paragraphs and Essays: A
    Worktext with Readings. 8th ed. Ed. Lee
    Brandon. Boston: Houghton, 2001. 249-50.
Shaw, Irwin. "The Girls in Their Summer
    Dresses." Paragraphs and Essays: A

```
Worktext with Readings. 8th ed. Ed. Lee
Brandon. Boston: Houghton, 2001.
310-15.
```

✳ Writer's Guidelines at a Glance: Reading for Writing

1. Underlining helps you to read with discrimination.

- Underline the main ideas in paragraphs.
- Underline the support for those ideas.
- Underline answers to questions that you bring to the reading assignment.
- Underline only the key words.

2. Annotating enables you to actively engage the reading material.

- Number parts if appropriate.
- Make comments according to your interests and needs.

3. Summarizing helps you concentrate on main ideas. A summary

- cites the author and title of the text.
- is usually shorter than the original by about two-thirds, although the exact reduction will vary depending on the content of the original.
- concentrates on the main ideas and includes details only infrequently.
- changes the original wording without changing the idea.
- does not evaluate the content or give an opinion in any way (even if the original contains an error in logic or fact).
- does not add ideas (even if the writer of the summary has an abundance of related information).
- does not include any personal comments by the writer of the summary (therefore, no use of *I*, referring to self).
- seldom contains quotations (although, if it does, only with quotation marks).
- includes some author tags ("says York," "according to York," or "the author explains") to remind the reader(s) that it is a summary of the material of another writer.

4. Two other types of text-based writing are

- the reaction, which shows how the reading relates to you, your experiences, and your attitudes; also, often a critique of the worth and logic of the piece.
- the two-part response, which includes a summary and a reaction that are separate.

5. Most ideas in text-based papers are developed in one or more of the following ways:

- explanation
- direct references
- quotations

6. Documenting is giving credit to borrowed ideas and words.

✳ 2

The Essay and Its Parts

✳ The Essay Defined

An **essay** is a group of paragraphs, each of which supports a controlling idea called a **thesis**. The number of paragraphs in an essay varies, but in college writing that number is likely to be between three and nine. Many college essays are about five paragraphs long, often because of the nature of the assignment and the length of time allowed, but there is no special significance in the number five.

Each paragraph in an essay is almost always one of three types:

1. The **introductory paragraph** presents the thesis, the controlling idea of the essay, much as a topic sentence presents the main idea of a paragraph.
2. The **paragraphs in the body of the essay** present evidence and reasoning—the support for the thesis of the essay.
3. The **concluding paragraph** provides an appropriate ending—often a restatement of or a reflection on the thesis.

Figure 2.1 shows the basic form of a typical essay, although the number of support paragraphs may vary.

Figure 2.1
Essay Form

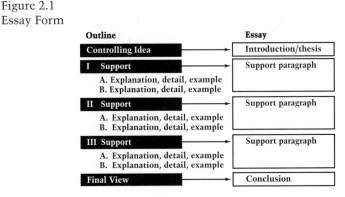

19

✳ A Sample Essay

The following essay was written by Leah, an inmate at a women's prison in California who enrolled in a small, low-cost college program. The parts of her essay are marked to show the organization of the paragraphs. Although only the final draft appears here, Leah's essay also provides the examples for the stages and techniques of the writing process discussed in Chapters 3 and 4.

Razor Wire Sweat Lodge

Leah

Introductory
paragraph
My Indian tribe is Pomo, one of twenty-one represented at this prison. I have always had tremendous interest in my ancestors and their customs, and in the cultures of all Indian tribes. The sacred sweat ceremony itself is at the center of my life. Here at prison it has taken on a special meaning. In fact, many women of other races here have also found peace within themselves as a result of participating with me and other **Thesis** Native Americans in the sweats. <u>Each Saturday we have a routine: we make preparations, we sweat, and we conclude with a post-sweat activity.</u>

Topic
sentence
<u>Before we sweat, we must prepare ourselves and the facility.</u> For twenty-four hours before the sweat, we fast. We do not eat anything and drink only water or juices, but if someone has a health problem, we will excuse her. As for clothing, we wear simple, loose dresses such as the prison-issued muu-muus. We bring tobacco ties, sage leaves, sweet grass, and sometimes a pipe. Preparing the facility is more complicated than preparing ourselves. About thirty-five lava rocks must be heated in a fire approximately

Support paragraph three hours before we start sweating. The wood for the fire has to be placed in a tepee shape around the pile of rocks and ignited. Once the fire is hot, we tend to the sweat lodge itself. Since we have no tarp to put on the sweat lodge frame, the state provides us with blankets. We use these to cover the lodge fully, draping it with about three layers and leaving an opening to the east. Finally we are ready to go inside. The preparation period is very important, but everyone looks forward to its being over.

Topic sentence From this point on through the ceremony, everything must be done according to rules. First we enter counterclockwise, and once inside we conduct all parts of the ceremony counterclockwise. There are four rounds in the sweat, each of which lasts about twenty to thirty minutes. We stress that no one **Support paragraph** should break our circle inside the sweat lodge, but it sometimes happens. Some women can't handle the steam and the heat, so we never make them stay. Those who do stay are free to participate in the singing and praying or not. The four rounds are similar. For each, six hot rocks are brought in, and six dippers of water are poured onto the rocks. The number six indicates the four directions and the sky and the ground. As someone finishes a prayer (usually in Sioux because our sponsor is a Sioux), she mentions her relatives, for this ceremony is also for others. Then another person follows. As sweet grass burns outside on the fire, we sit in the hot steam and rub sage leaves on our bodies for purification. We maintain

ourselves with humility during the whole
sweat.

Topic
sentence

When the sweat is over, we enter the
final phase. We come out and throw our tobacco
ties into the fire pit, and the smoke takes
our prayers to the sky. Then we hose ourselves
down with plenty of cold water and open the

Support
paragraph

refreshments we brought. Once we've eaten and
changed our clothes, we start dismantling the
sweat. The blankets have to be taken off the
same way they were put up and then folded
carefully. The leftover wood has to be put
away, and the blankets and wood must be
covered. Any garbage that's been left around
is thrown into the Dumpster. Then we lock the
gate to our facility and bid farewell.

Using a sweat lodge is a custom of most
Indian tribes. Certain Indian tribes go about
it differently from others, but in here when
we are together in the lodge, we feel like

Concluding
paragraph

one whole being. Each week we look forward to
this ceremony. It helps us cope better with
the prison system. After it's over, we feel
physically refreshed, clean, and peaceful.

✳ The Thesis Defined

If you tell a friend you are about to write an essay, be prepared for
the question, "What are you writing about?" If you answer, "Public
schools," your friend will probably be satisfied with the answer but
not very interested. The problem is that the phrase *public schools*
doesn't suggest a focus or direction. It just indicates your subject,
not what you are going to do with it. An effective controlling statement, called the *thesis of the essay,* has both a subject and a treatment. The **subject** is what you intend to write about. The **treatment**
is what you intend to do with your subject.

Glendora High School offers a well-balanced academic program.
<u>subject</u>   <u>treatment</u>

✳ Sources for the Thesis

The thesis of an essay can come from any of several places. You may generate it early on through prewriting techniques, you may develop it from something you have read, or you may be assigned a topic. In any case, you need to work on your thesis statement—just that one sentence—until you have developed an interesting subject and a well-focused treatment. Your working thesis may be a bit different from the one you finally use in your essay, but it can easily be reworded once you begin writing and revising.

✳ Writing the Thesis

An effective thesis includes a treatment that can be developed with supporting information. An ineffective thesis presents a treatment that is vague, too broad, or too narrow.

VAGUE   <u>Public schools</u> <u>are great.</u>
         subject   treatment

BETTER   <u>Public schools</u> <u>do as well academically as private</u>
         subject   treatment
         <u>schools, according to statistics.</u> (made more specific)

TOO BROAD   <u>Public schools</u> <u>are having trouble.</u> (trouble with
             subject   treatment
             what?)

BETTER   <u>Bidwell Elementary School</u> <u>is too crowded.</u>
         subject   treatment
         (limiting the idea of trouble)

TOO NARROW   <u>American public schools</u> <u>were first established</u>
             subject   treatment
             <u>in Philadelphia in 1779.</u> (only a fact)

Exercise 1 Evaluating Topic Sentences

In the following theses, underline and label the subjects (S) and treatments (T). Also judge each one as effective (E) or ineffective (I).

EXAMPLE ___I___   <u>Basketball</u> <u>is an interesting sport.</u>
                              S   T

_____   1. Students who cheat in school may be trying
                        to relieve certain emotional pressures.

_____   2. Shakespeare was an Elizabethan writer.

_____   3. The quarterback in football and the general
                        of an army are alike in significant ways.

_____   4. Animals use color chiefly for protection.

_____   5. Portland is a city in Oregon.

_____   6. Life in the ocean has distinct realms.

_____   7. Rome has had a glorious and tragic history.

_____   8. Boston is the capital of Massachusetts.

_____   9. The word *macho* has a special meaning
                        to the Hispanic community.

_____ 10. The history of plastics is exciting.

Exercise 2 Writing Topic Sentences

Convert each of the following subjects into an effective thesis.

1. Bumper stickers _____

   _____

2. Rudeness _____

   _____

3. The true character of my neighbor _____

   _____

4. Many homeless people _____

   _____

5. Being able to use a computer_____

   _____

6. Dieting _____

7. The basic forms of jazz and classical music _____

8. Educated citizens _____

9. The required labeling of rock music albums_____

10. Smoking _____

❋ Patterns of Support for the Thesis

If the foundation of an effective essay is a strong thesis—one with a specific subject and a well-defined treatment—the strength of the essay is in the support. Whether that support comes from research or personal experience, it will almost certainly be suggested by the treatment imposed on the subject. After settling on a thesis, you should pose two questions:

1. What kinds of information will best support or explain my thesis?
2. How should I divide and present that supporting information?

The way you choose to divide and present your information will determine the organization of your support paragraphs.

Among the most common forms of dividing and organizing ideas are the following:

- Descriptive narration (telling a story with relevant descriptions)

    Division: parts of the story
     I. Situation
     II. Conflict
     III. Struggle
     IV. Outcome
     V. Meaning

- Analysis by division (examining the parts of a unit; for example, a pencil can be divided into an eraser, a wooden barrel, and a lead core with a point at the end)

  Division: parts of the unit
  I. First part
  II. Second part
  III. Third part

- Process analysis (how to do something or how something was done)

  Division: preparation and steps
  I. Preparation
  II. Steps
    A. Step 1
    B. Step 2
    C. Step 3
    D. Step 4

- Cause and effect

  Division: causes or effects (sometimes mixed)
  I. Cause (or effect) 1
  II. Cause (or effect) 2
  III. Cause (or effect) 3

Other patterns of developing an essay include exemplification, comparison and contrast, definition, and argument. All of these forms are presented individually in Chapters 5 through 12. Although a single form is often dominant at either the paragraph or short essay level, a rich combination of forms is common.

✳ Special Paragraphs Within the Essay

Introductions

A good introductory paragraph does many things. It attracts the reader's interest, states or points toward the thesis, and moves the reader smoothly into the support, or body, paragraphs. Here are some introductory methods:

- A direct statement of the thesis
- Background
- Definition of term(s)

- Quotation(s)
- A shocking statement
- Question(s)
- A combination of two or more methods in this list

You should not decide that some of the methods are good and some are bad. Indeed, all are valid, and the most common one is the last, the combination. Use the approach that best fits each essay. Resist the temptation to use the same kind of introduction in every essay you write.

Each of the following statements is an introductory paragraph. The thesis is the same in all of them, yet each uses a different introductory method. Notice the great variety here.

Direct Statement of Thesis

Anyone on the road in any city near midnight on Friday and Saturday is among dangerous people. They're not the product of the witching hour; they're the product of the **Subject** "happy hour." They're called drunk drivers. <u>These threats</u> **Treatment** <u>to our lives and limbs need to be controlled by federal laws with strong provisions.</u>

Background

In one four-year period in California (2001–2005), 18,942 people were injured and 6,974 were killed by drunk drivers. Each year, the same kinds of figures come in from all our states. The state laws vary. The federal government does virtually nothing. Drunk driving has reached the point of being a national problem of huge proportions. **Subject** <u>This slaughter of innocent citizens should be stopped by</u> **Treatment** <u>following the lead of many other nations and passing federal legislation with strong provisions.</u>

Definition

Here's a recipe. Take two thousand pounds of plastic, rubber, and steel, pour in ten gallons of gas, and start the engine. Then take one human being of two hundred pounds of flesh, blood, and bones, pour in two glasses of beer in one hour, and put him or her behind the wheel. Mix the two together, and the result may be a drunken **Subject** driver ready to cause death and destruction. <u>This problem</u>

Treatment   of drunk driving <u>can and should be controlled by federal</u>
<u>legislation with strong provisions.</u>

Quotation

The National Highway Traffic Safety Administration
has stated that 50 percent of all fatal accidents involve
intoxicated drivers and about "75 percent of those drivers have a Blood Alcohol Content of .10 percent or
greater." That kind of information is widely known, yet
Subject   the carnage on the highways continues. <u>This problem of</u>
Treatment   <u>drunk driving should be addressed by a federal law with</u>
<u>strict provisions.</u>

Shocking Statement and Questions

Almost 60,000 Americans were killed in the Vietnam
War. What other war kills more than that number every
four years? Give up? It's the war with drunk drivers. The
war in Vietnam ended more than three decades ago, but
Subject   our DUI war goes on, and the drunks are winning. <u>This</u>
Treatment   <u>deadly conflict should be controlled by federal laws</u>
<u>with strong provisions.</u>

Questions and a Definition

What is a drunk driver? In California it's a person with a
blood alcohol content of .08 percent or more who is operating a motor vehicle. What do those drivers do? Some of
them kill. Every year more than 16,000 people nationwide
die. Those are easy questions. The difficult one is, What
Subject   can be done? One answer is clear: <u>Drunk drivers should</u>
Treatment   <u>be controlled by federal laws with strong provisions.</u>

All these introductory methods are effective. Some others, however, are ineffective because they are too vague to carry the thesis or
because they carry the thesis in a mechanical way. The mechanical
approach may be direct and explicit, but it usually destroys the
reader's imagination and interest.

> Vague   The purpose of this essay is to write about the need
> for strong national laws against drunk driving.
>
> Mechanical   I will now write a paper about the need for strong
> national laws against drunk driving.

The length of an introduction can vary, but the typical length for an introduction to a student essay is three to five sentences. If your introduction is shorter than three, be certain that it conveys all that you want to say. If it is longer than five, be certain that it only introduces and does not try to expand on ideas. That function is reserved for the body paragraphs; a long and complicated introduction may make your essay top-heavy.

Exercise 3 Writing Introductory Paragraphs

Pick one of the following theses (altering it a bit to suit your own ideas, if you like) and write two different introductory paragraphs for it, each one featuring a different method. Underline the thesis in each paragraph, and label the subject and treatment parts.

1. Marriages come in different shapes and sizes.
2. Career choices are greatly influenced by a person's background.
3. *Friendship* is just one word, but friends are of different kinds.
4. The spirit of sports has been corrupted by money.
5. Sexual harassment at work often goes unreported for practical reasons.

Support Paragraphs

Support paragraphs, also called **developmental paragraphs,** form the body of an essay and provide information and reasoning that justify the thesis presented in the paragraph of introduction.

The following paragraph is both a definition and an example of the developmental paragraph:

Topic sentence	The developmental paragraph contains three parts: the subject, the topic sentence, and the support. The subject
Support	is what you will write about. It is likely to be broad and must be focused or qualified for specific treatment.
Support	The topic sentence contains both the subject and the treatment—what you will do with the subject. It carries the central idea to which everything else in the paragraph is subordinated. For example, the first sentence of this paragraph is a topic sentence. Even when not stated,
Support	the topic sentence as an underlying idea unifies the paragraph. The support is the evidence or reasoning by which

a topic sentence is developed. It comes in several basic patterns and serves any of the four forms of expression: narration, description, exposition, and argumentation. These forms, which are usually combined in writing, will be presented with both student and professional examples in the following chapters. The developmental paragraph, therefore, is a group of sentences, each with **Concluding** the function of supporting a controlling idea called the **sentence** topic sentence.

Incompleteness of support is more common among beginning writers than is overdevelopment of support. Besides having enough support, be sure that the points are presented in the best possible sequence.

Consider the following paragraph. Is it complete? Does the writer make the main idea clear and provide adequate support for it? Are the ideas in the right order?

> A cat's tail is a good barometer of its intentions. By various movements of its tail a cat will signal many of its wants. Other movements indicate its attitudes. An excited or aggressively aroused cat will whip its entire tail back and forth.

At first glance, this paragraph seems complete. It begins with a concise topic sentence telling us that a cat's tail is "a good barometer of its intentions." It adds information of a general nature in the following two sentences. Then it presents a supporting example about the aggressively aroused cat. But the paragraph is not explicit; it contains insufficient supporting material for the opening generalization. The paragraph leaves the reader with too much information to fill in. What are some other ways that cats communicate their intentions with their tails? How do they communicate specific wishes or desires? Is their communication effective? If the passage is to answer these questions that may come into the reader's mind, it must present more material to support the beginning generalization. The original paragraph that follows begins with a concise topic sentence that is then supported with details.

> A cat's tail is a good barometer of its intentions. An excited or aggressively aroused cat will whip its entire tail back and forth. When I talk to Sam, he holds up his end of the conversation by occasionally flicking the tip of his tail. Mother cats move their tails back and forth to invite their kittens to play. A kitten raises its tail perpendicularly to beg for attention; older cats may do so

to beg for food. When your cat holds its tail aloft while criss-crossing in front of you, it is trying to say. "Follow me"—usually to the kitchen or, more precisely, to the refrigerator. Unfortunately, many cats have lost their tails in refrigerator doors as a consequence.

—*Michael W. Fox, "What Is Your Pet Trying to Tell You?"*

We can strengthen our understanding of good support by analyzing the structure of our model paragraph, putting to use the information we have assimilated to this point in the discussion. The paragraph begins with the highest generalization (the main idea in the topic sentence): "A cat's tail is a good barometer of its intentions." It follows immediately with six major supporting statements and ends with a final sentence to add humor to the writing. If we place this material in outline form, we can easily see the recurrent pattern in the flow of thought from general to particular.

TOPIC SENTENCE (HIGHEST GENERALIZATION)	A cat's tail is a good barometer of its intentions.
MAJOR SUPPORT	A. An excited or aggressively aroused cat will whip its entire tail back and forth.
MAJOR SUPPORT	B. When I talk to Sam, he holds up his end of the conversation by occasionally flicking the tip of his tail.
MAJOR SUPPORT	C. Mother cats move their tails back and forth to invite their kittens to play.
MAJOR SUPPORT	D. A kitten raises its tail perpendicularly to beg for attention;
MAJOR SUPPORT	E. older cats may do so to beg for food.
MAJOR SUPPORT	F. When your cat holds its tail aloft while crisscrossing in front of you, it is trying to say, "Follow me"—usually to the kitchen or, more precisely, to the refrigerator.
CONCLUDING SENTENCE (ADDED FOR HUMOR)	Unfortunately, many cats have lost their tails in refrigerator doors as a consequence.

Figure 2.2
Paragraph Frames

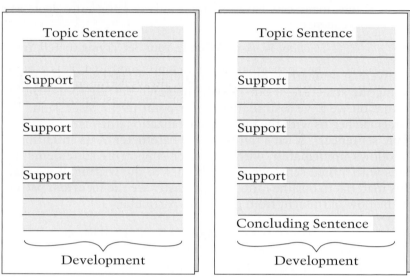

Frame A   **Frame B**

Basic Frames

Two effective frames of conventional paragraph structure are shown in Figure 2.2. Frame A merely states the controlling idea, the topic sentence, and develops it; Frame B adds a concluding sentence following the development. Two other forms—the paragraph with an unstated but implied topic sentence and the paragraph with the topic sentence at the end of the paragraph—are used less frequently in college writing.

Following is an example of Frame A:

Pity, Anger, and Achievement Performance

It is generally thought that pity and sympathy are "good" emotions and that anger is a "bad" emotion. However, attribution theorists have pointed out that the consequences of these emotional expressions are complex. In one investigation, Graham (1984) gave subjects (twelve-year-old children) false failure feedback during an achievement task. For some children, this was accompanied by the remark: "I feel sorry for you" as well as

(left margin labels: **Topic sentence** / **Support**)

body postures and facial gestures that accompany sympathy (head down, hands folded, etc.). To other students, the experimenter said: "I am angry with you." Students receiving the pity feedback tended to blame the failure on themselves (low ability) and their performance declined. On the other hand, students receiving anger feedback attributed their failure to lack of effort and

Support their performance subsequently increased. <u>This is not to advocate that sympathy is always detrimental and anger always facilitative.</u> Rather, the consequences of feedback depend on how that feedback is construed and what it means to the recipient of the communication. Other kinds of feedback, such as praise for success at an easy task and excessive and unsolicited helping, also tend to convey that the student is "unable" and therefore have some negative consequences.

—Seymour Feshbach and Bernard Weiner, Personality

Here is an example of Frame B:

Primitive Methods of Lie Detection

Topic <u>Throughout history there have been efforts to distinguish</u>
sentence <u>the guilty from the innocent and to tell the liars from the</u>
Support <u>truthful.</u> For example, <u>a method of lie detection practiced</u> <u>in Asia</u> involved giving those suspected of a crime a handful of raw rice to chew. After chewing for some time, the persons were instructed to spit out the rice. The innocent person was anticipated to do this easily, whereas the guilty party was expected to have grains of rice sticking to the roof of the mouth and tongue. This technique relied on the increased sympathetic nervous system activity in the presumably fearful and guilty person. This activity would result in the drying up of saliva that, in turn, would

Support cause grains of rice to stick in the mouth. <u>A similar but</u> <u>more frightening technique</u> involved placing a heated knife blade briefly against the tongue, another method used for criminal detection. An innocent person would not be burned while the guilty party would immediately feel pain, again because of the relative dryness of the

Concluding mouth. <u>Many of these methods relied (unknowingly) on</u>
sentence <u>the basic physiological principles that also guided the</u> <u>creation of the polygraph.</u>

—Seymour Feshbach and Bernard Weiner, Personality

Exercise 4 Analyzing a Paragraph

1. Is the following paragraph developed according to Frame A (topic sentence/development) or Frame B (topic sentence/development/ concluding sentence)?
2. Identify the parts of the paragraph frame by underlining the topic sentence and the concluding sentence, if any, and by annotating the support in the left margin. Use the two example paragraphs as models.

> But now I can say that I am a Japanese-American. It means I have a place here in this country, too. I have a place here on the East Coast, where our neighbor is so much a part of our family that my mother never passes her house at night without glancing at the lights to see if she is home and safe; where my parents have hauled hundreds of pounds of rocks from fields and arduously planted Christmas trees and blueberries, lilacs, asparagus, and crab apples, where my father still dreams of angling a stream to a new bed so that he can dig a pond in the field and fill it with water and fish. "The neighbors already came for their Christmas tree?" he asks in December. "Did they like it? Did they like it?"
>
> —*Kesaya E. Noda, "Growing Up Asian in America"*

Exercise 5 Analyzing a Paragraph

1. Is the following paragraph developed according to Frame A (topic sentence/development) or Frame B (topic sentence/development/ concluding sentence)?
2. Identify the parts of the paragraph frame by underlining the topic sentence and the concluding sentence, if any, and by annotating the support in the left margin. Use the two example paragraphs as models.

> I can see myself today as a person historically defined by law and custom as being forever alien. Being neither "free white," nor "African," our people in California were deemed "aliens, ineligible for citizenship," no matter how long they intended to stay here. Aliens ineligible for citizenship were prohibited from owning, buying, or leasing land. They did not and could not belong here. The voice in me remembers that I am always a Japanese-American in the eyes of many. A third-generation German-American is an American. A third-generation Japanese-American

is a Japanese-American. Being Japanese means being a danger to the country during the war and knowing how to use chopsticks. I wear this history on my face.

—*Kesaya E. Noda*, "Growing Up Asian in America"

Conclusions

Your concluding paragraph should give the reader the feeling that you have said all you want to say about your subject. Like introductory paragraphs, concluding paragraphs are of various types. Here are some effective ways of concluding a paper:

- Conclude with a final paragraph or sentence that is a logical part of the body of the paper; that is, it functions as part of the support. In the following example, there is no formal conclusion. This form is more common in the published essay than in the student essay.

  One day he hit me. He said he was sorry and even cried, but I could not forgive him. We got a divorce. It took me a while before I could look back and see what the causes really were, but by then it was too late to make any changes.

  —*Maria Campos*, "A Divorce with Reasons"

- Conclude with a restatement of the thesis in slightly different words, perhaps pointing out its significance or making applications.

  Don't blame it on the referee. Don't even blame it on the fight managers. Put the blame where it belongs—on the prevailing mores that regard prize fighting as a perfectly proper enterprise and vehicle of entertainment. No one doubts that many people enjoy prize fighting and will miss it if it should be thrown out. And that is precisely the point.

  —*Norman Cousins*, "Who Killed Benny Paret?"

- Conclude with a review of the main points of the discussion— a kind of summary. This is appropriate only if the complexity of the essay makes a summary necessary.

  As we have been made all too aware lately in this country, the more energy we conserve now, the more we'll have for the future.

The same holds true for skiing. So take the Soft Path of energy conservation as you ski. You'll not only be able to make longer nonstop runs, but you'll have more energy to burn on the dance floor.

—Carl Wingus, "Conserving Energy as You Ski"

- Conclude with an anecdote related to the thesis.

Over the harsh traffic sounds of motors and horns and blaring radios came the faint whang-whang of a would-be musician with a beat-up guitar and a money-drop hat turned up at his feet. It all reminded me of when I had first experienced the conglomeration of things that now assailed my senses. This jumbled mixture of things both human and nonhuman was, in fact, the reason I had come to live here. Then it was different and exciting. Later it was the reason I was leaving.

—Brian Maxwell, "Leaving Los Angeles"

- Conclude with a quotation related to the thesis.

He [Johnny Cash] had, of course, long since attained a legendary stature few performers ever achieved. Terri Clark, a country songstress two generations removed, captured a sense of it in a statement released Friday. "What really made him stand out, more than the back-beats, the TV shows, the hit records, was how he stood up for the little people, the way he believed in the right things. . . . He was a beacon for both musical and personal integrity, and he set a bar most of us can only gaze at."

—Dave Tianen, "A Music Legend Fades to Black"

There are also many ineffective ways of concluding a paper. Do not conclude with the following:

- a summary when a summary is unnecessary
- a complaint about the assignment or an apology about the quality of the work
- an afterthought—that is, something you forgot to discuss in the body of the paper
- a tagged conclusion—that is, a sentence beginning with such phrases as *In conclusion, To conclude, I would like to conclude this discussion,* or *Last but not least*
- a conclusion that raises additional problems that should have been settled during the discussion.

The conclusion is an integral part of the essay and is often a reflection of the introduction. If you have trouble with the conclusion, reread your introduction. Then work for a roundness or completeness in the whole paper.

Exercise 6 Writing a Conclusion

For Exercise 3, you wrote two introductions. Select the better one, consider the basic information you would probably use for support (jotting down a few ideas if you like), and then write a simple conclusion of three to five sentences. This exercise demonstrates that the conclusion connects with the introduction, is a consequence of the development of the essay, and ends on a note of finality. In your regular assignments, you will not write your conclusion until after you have written the paragraphs of support.

✳ Writer's Guidelines at a Glance: The Essay and Its Parts

1. An **essay** is a group of paragraphs, each of which supports a controlling statement called a **thesis.**
2. Each paragraph in an essay is almost always one of three types: introductory, support (developmental), or concluding.
3. An effective thesis has both a subject and a treatment. The **subject** is what you intend to write about. The **treatment** is what you intend to do with your subject.

   EXAMPLE   <u>Bidwell Elementary School</u> <u>is too crowded.</u>
                      subject   treatment

4. An effective thesis presents a treatment that can be developed with supporting information.
5. An ineffective thesis is vague, too broad, or too narrow.
6. Supporting information is presented in one of the following patterns—such as descriptive narration, analysis by division, process analysis, cause and effect, exemplification, comparison and contrast, definition, and argument—or in a combination of patterns.
7. A good **introductory paragraph** attracts the reader's interest, states or points toward the thesis, and moves the reader smoothly into the support, or body, paragraphs.

8. Introductory methods include a direct statement of the thesis, background, definition of term(s), quotation(s), a shocking statement, question(s), and a combination of two or more methods in this list.

9. **Support paragraphs,** also called **developmental paragraphs,** form the body of an essay and provide information and reasoning that justify the thesis presented in the paragraph of introduction. The developmental paragraph contains three parts: the subject, the topic sentence, and the support. It may also have a concluding sentence.

10. Your **concluding paragraph** should give the reader the feeling that you have said all you want to say about your subject.

11. Some effective methods of concluding are restating the thesis in slightly different words, perhaps pointing out its significance or applying it; reviewing the main points; presenting an anecdote related to the thesis; and using a quotation.

✳ 3

The Writing Process:
Prewriting

Chapter 2 focused on organizing and writing an essay. However, it stopped short of presenting an overall plan for completing a specific writing assignment. The reason for that omission is simple: Each assignment has its own guidelines that vary according to the kind of topic, the source of ideas, the time permitted, the conditions for writing (especially in or outside class), and the purpose. Obviously, if one is to use a system, it must be flexible because a technique that is an asset for one assignment may be a burden for another. Therefore, a good writer should know numerous techniques, treating each as a tool that can be used when needed. All of these tools are in the same box, one labeled "The Writing Process."

✳ The Writing Process Defined

The writing process consists of strategies that can help you proceed from your purpose or initial idea to a final developed essay. Those strategies can be divided into prewriting techniques and writing stages. Using prewriting techniques, you explore, experiment, gather information, formulate your thesis, and develop and organize your support. In the writing stages, you write a first draft, revise your draft as many times as necessary, and edit your writing. For the typical college writing assignment, the writing process looks like the following:

Prewriting
- Explore, experiment, and gather information
- Write the controlling idea
- Organize and develop support

Writing
- Draft, revise, and edit

39

A flexible set of steps is included in the Writing Process Worksheet on page xxi. It can be enlarged, photocopied, and submitted with your assignment, if your instructor asks you to do so.

Prewriting is discussed in this chapter, and writing is discussed in Chapter 4. The examples come from Leah's essay, "Razor Wire Sweat Lodge."

✳ Prewriting Strategies

Prewriting strategies include freewriting, brainstorming and listing, clustering, composing the thesis, and outlining.

Freewriting

Freewriting is an exercise that its originator, Peter Elbow, has called "babbling in print." In freewriting, you write without stopping, letting your ideas tumble forth. You do not concern yourself with the fundamentals of writing, such as punctuation and spelling. Freewriting is an adventure into your memory and imagination. It is discovery, invention, and exploration. If you are at a loss for words on your subject, write down a comment such as "I don't know what is coming next" or "blah, blah, blah," and continue when relevant words come. It is important to continue writing. Freewriting immediately eliminates the blank page and thereby helps you break through an emotional barrier, but that is not the only benefit. The words that you sort through in that fashion will include some you can use. You can then underline or circle those words and even add notes on the side so that the freewriting continues to grow even after its initial, spontaneous expression.

The way you proceed depends on the type of assignment:

> working with a topic of your choice
> working from a restricted list of topics
> working with a prescribed topic

Working with the topic of your choice gives you the greatest freedom of exploration. You would probably select a subject that interests you and freewrite about it, allowing your mind to wander among its many parts, perhaps mixing fact and fantasy, direct experience, and hearsay. A freewriting about music might uncover areas of special interest and knowledge, such as jazz or folk rock, that you would want to pursue further in freewriting or other prewriting strategies.

Working from a restricted list requires a more focused freewriting. With the list, you can, of course, experiment with several topics to discover what is most suitable for you. If, for example, "career choice," "career preparation," "career guidance," and "career prospects" are on the restricted list, you would probably select one and freewrite about it. If it works well for you, you would probably proceed with the next step of your prewriting. If you are not satisfied with what you uncover in freewriting, you would explore another item from the restricted list.

When working with a prescribed topic, you focus on a particular topic and try to restrict your freewriting to its boundaries. If your topic specifies a division of a subject area such as "political involvement of your generation," then you would tie those key words to your own information, critical thinking, and imaginative responses. If the topic is restricted to, let's say, your reaction to a particular reading selection such as a poem, then that poem would give you a framework for freewriting about your own experiences, creations, and opinions. An analysis of the piece would probably include underlining pertinent ideas, annotating it (writing in the margins), and even taking notes on it. Freewriting can help you get words on paper to generate topics, develop new insights, and explore ideas.

Freewriting can lead to other stages of prewriting and writing, and it can also provide content for details and insights as you develop your topic. Let's back up and see how Leah used freewriting to begin exploring her ideas for her essay. Leah was assigned to write a personal essay of 500 to 800 words. Her instructor suggested she concentrate on a recent development or prison event that changed her life, for better or worse.

Several topics interested her. There was the problem of overcrowding: she lived in an institution built for 900 inmates, and the population was now 2,200. She also considered education. After spending some time in routine prison work and aimless activities, she had discovered school and found it highly satisfying. And then there were the accomplishments of her Native American friends at the prison. After years of arguing their case, they had finally obtained permission from the institution to build a sweat lodge for religious purposes, and it was now in operation. That was a subject she knew well, and it was one for which she held the most enthusiasm.

Leah started freewriting, which enabled her to probe her memory and see which aspects of the subject she was most interested in. She wrote without stopping, as she liberated and associated the many thoughts she had on the subject of *sweat lodge.* Following is some of Leah's freewriting.

For several years I have wanted to worship in the way that I did when I was on the reservation. These people here at prison were discriminating against me, I thought. I knew that the other people here could go to the chaplain and to the chapel and they could do so without people complaining or going to any bother. I didn't know why they did not allow me to follow my own religious preference. Then I talked to the other Indian sisters here at prison and they told me that they had been working for many years to get a sweat lodge. I started working with them. It took years of work, but it is worth it for

Have sweat lodge now

now we have a sweat lodge where we can go for our ceremonies. It makes me feel good. I look forward to it. I have used it once a week for most of the last year. When I am nervous and when things are tense on the prison grounds, I think about the sweat lodge and just thinking about it gives me some peace. Then when I go there and sweat for a period of time I seem to feel that I am leaving the prison grounds and I am at peace with the

Ceremony important

universe. It is a ceremony that is important to me and also to the prison. We even have women who are not Indians who are interested and we teach them about Indian ways and we all learn from what we do. What else is there to say. I could go on and on. That is what I have to say. I love the sweat lodge which we call the sweats. I think it is the most important thing in my life now. I used to be bitter toward the prison for denying me my

At peace   `rights, but now I am even `<u>`at peace`</u>` with them--`
`most of the time. I remember when we were`
`trying to get approval and . . . [partial]`

After her freewriting session, Leah examined what she had written for possible ideas to develop for a writing assignment. As she recognized those ideas, she underlined key words and phrases and made a few notes in the margins. By reading only the underlined words, you can understand what is important to Leah; she did not need to underline whole sentences.

In addition to putting words on that dreaded blank sheet of paper, Leah discovered that she had quite a lot to say about the sweat lodge and that she had selected a favorable topic to develop. The entire process took no more than five minutes. Had she found only a few ideas or no promising ideas at all, she might have freewritten on another topic. In going back over her work she saw some errors, especially in wording and sentence structure, but she did not correct them because the purpose of freewriting is discovery, not revising or correcting grammar, punctuation, and spelling. She was confident that she could continue with the process of writing a paper.

Exercise 1 Freewriting

Freewrite for a few minutes on one of the following topics. After you finish freewriting, take two minutes or so to mark the key words and phrases. Then make a few notations if you find some promising ideas that could be developed.

An event that was important to you in your youth
A concert, a movie, or a television program
Types of radio stations
Drug abuse—causes, effects, a friend with a problem
Gang membership—causes, effects, an experience
Ways of disciplining children
A family reunion, wedding, funeral, or graduation
A great or terrible party
A bad or good day at school
Why a college education is important
How music (rock, rap, country) affects or reveals the attitudes
   of its fans
Your most memorable job
A date from hell or heaven

Brainstorming and Listing

Brainstorming is a strategy for coming up with fresh, new ideas in a hurry. What key words and phrases pop into your mind when you think about your topic? One effective way to get started brainstorming is to ask the big six questions about your subject area: *Who?* *What?* *Where?* *When?* *Why?* and *How?* Then let your mind run free as you jot down answers in single entries or lists. Using the big six questions also helps you begin to organize ideas for your writing. Some of the big six questions may not fit, and some may be more important than others, depending on the purpose of your writing. For example, if you were writing about the causes of an accident, the *Why?* question could be more important than the others. If you were concerned with how to succeed in college, the *How?* question would predominate. If you were writing in response to a reading selection, you would confine your thinking to questions related to the content of the reading selection.

Whatever the focus of the six questions, the result is likely to be numerous ideas that will provide information for continued exploration and development of your topic. Thus your pool of information for writing widens and deepens.

An alternative to the big six questions approach is simply to make a list of words and phrases related to your subject area or specific topic.

Leah continued with the subject of the sweat lodge, and her topic tightened to focus on particular areas. Although she could have listed the annotations and the words she underlined in her freewriting, she instead used the big six questions for her framework.

Who?	American Indian inmates and others
What?	sweat lodge, how it was started, the politics, the ceremonies
Where?	California Institution for Women—off the yard
When?	1989, before, after, long time in planning and building
Why?	spiritual, physical, self-esteem, educational
How?	preparation, steps

Leah's listing might have taken this form:

Sweat Lodge	Ceremony	Result
Problems in building it	Preparation	Relaxed
	Blankets	Spiritually clean

Reasons	Rocks	Peaceful
Fairness	Fire	
Who helped	Water	
Time to build	Tobacco and	
	sweet grass	
	Sweating	
	Passing pipe	
	Tearing down	

Exercise 2 Brainstorming or Listing

Brainstorm or make a list for the topic that interested you in Exercise 1.

Clustering

Clustering (also called *mapping*) is yet another prewriting technique. Start by double-bubbling your topic; that is, write it down in the middle of the page and draw a double circle around it, like the hub of a wheel. Then respond to the question, "What comes to mind?"

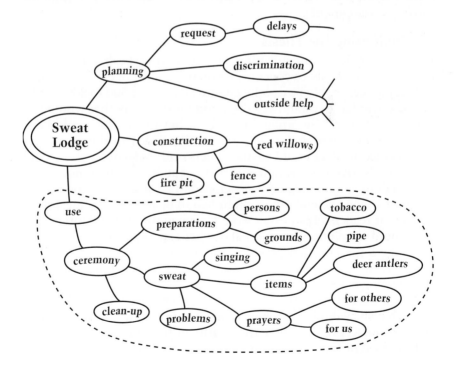

Single-bubble other ideas on spokes radiating from the hub. Any bubble can lead to another bubble or to numerous bubbles in the same way. This strategy is sometimes used instead of or before making an outline to organize and develop ideas.

The more specific the topic inside the double bubble, the fewer the number of spokes that will radiate from it. For example, a topic such as "high school dropouts" would have more spokes than "reasons for dropping out of high school."

Leah's cluster on her topic of the prison sweat lodge is shown on page 45.

Notice that after completing her basic cluster, Leah went back and drew a broken boundary around subclusters that offered encouraging areas for focus. Some subclusters, usually with further clustering to provide details, can be as good as an outline in offering structure and content for the development of an essay.

Exercise 3 Clustering

Make a cluster on the topic you chose in Exercise 1. After you finish, draw broken boundaries around subclusters that have potential for further development.

Composing the Thesis

After freewriting, brainstorming, and clustering, Leah was ready to focus. She was ready to concentrate on one aspect of her larger topic that could reasonably be developed into an essay of 500 to 800 words. She also wanted to establish a direction for the essay that would target her audience, who knew little about her topic. She would have to explain her topic in detail as a controlling idea, or thesis, so that uninformed readers could easily understand. Moreover, she would avoid any Native American words that her audience might not know. Although the sweat lodge was developed in an atmosphere of controversy in which she and others often had to be persuasive, she anticipated that readers of her essay would be open-minded and interested. She would simply inform them about her experience with the sweat lodge, giving a personal perspective. She would also have to avoid using prison slang because this essay was for an assignment in a college writing class.

Leah made three attempts to write a sentence with both a subject (what she would write about) and a treatment (what she would do with her subject). She wanted the treatment to be just right, not vague or too broad or too narrow.

I want to explain how we use the sweats and why.

Using the prison sweat lodge involves specific practices that contribute to my well-being.

Subject	I want to discuss the <u>prison sweat lodge</u>, <u>what we</u>
Treatment	<u>do in the preparation period</u>, <u>what we do when</u> <u>we're inside for the ceremony</u>, and <u>what we do</u> <u>afterward</u>.

Her third attempt satisfied her, and the statement became her thesis. Later she would reword it.

Exercise 4 Writing a Thesis

After consulting your freewriting, brainstorming or listing, and clustering, write a thesis. Label the subject and treatment parts.

Outlining

Outlining is the tool that most people think of in connection with organizing. Outlining does basically the same thing that listing and clustering do. Outlining divides the controlling idea into sections of support material, divides those sections further, and establishes sequence.

An outline is a kind of framework, and it can be used in two ways. It can indicate the plan for a paragraph or an essay you intend to write. It can also show the organization of a passage you are reading. The outline of a reading passage and the outline as a plan for writing are identical in form. If you intend to write a summary of a reading selection, then a single outline might be used for both purposes.

The two main outline forms are the **sentence outline** (each entry is a complete sentence) and the **topic outline** (each entry is a key word or phrase). The topic outline is more common in writing paragraphs and essays.

In the following topic outline, notice first how the parts are arranged on the page: the indentations, the number and letter sequences, the punctuation, and the placement of words. Then read the outline and see how the ideas relate to one another.

Main idea (usually the topic sentence for a paragraph or the thesis for an essay)

I. Major support
   A. Minor support
      1. Explanation, detail, example
      2. Explanation, detail, example

   B. Minor support
      1. Explanation, detail, example
      2. Explanation, detail, example
   II. Major support
      A. Minor support
         1. Explanation, detail, example
         2. Explanation, detail, example
      B. Minor support
         1. Explanation, detail, example
         2. Explanation, detail, example

Leah's next task was to organize her material. For this strategy, she went back to her bubble cluster, which she had divided into "planning," "construction," and "use." She had already decided she wanted to work with the "use" aspect and explain it from her perspective. Therefore, she focused on only one part of the cluster—the part indicated by the broken boundary line.

She might have started to write a first draft at this point, but instead she decided she wanted to recall and organize more detail, so she began an outline. She used her own memory and private reference sources for information. If she had been working on a reading-related topic, she would have gone back to the reading. If she had been working on a topic subject to research, she would have consulted library sources.

Leah's outline shows the relationship of ideas, suggests ways to divide the essay according to her thesis, and indicates support. The divisions are Preparation, Ceremony, and Ceremony completion and site restoration. Those items are Leah's Roman-numeral headings.

   I. Preparation
      A. Fasting
         1. Duration
         2. Only water or juices
      B. Heat rocks
         1. Thirty to fifty
         2. Build fire
      C. Set up lodge
         1. Permission from sponsor
         2. Cover framework

II. Ceremony
    A. Movement
        1. Going and coming
        2. Passing sacred objects
    B. Establishing attitude
    C. Sweating
    D. Praying and singing
    E. Purification rites
        1. Tobacco ties
        2. Sage
        3. Sweet grass
III. Ceremony completion and site restoration
    A. Personal
        1. Water down
        2. Eat and drink
        3. Change
    B. Site
        1. Remove and store blankets
        2. Move rocks

Exercise 5 Completing Outlines

Fill in the missing parts of the following outlines. It may be helpful to ask, in each case, whether you are dealing with time, examples, causes, effects, parts, or steps. The answers will vary, depending on your individual experiences and views.

1. Borrowing   is the mother of trouble.
   subject   treatment

    I. Received five credit cards in mail

   II. Saw numerous commercials on television

       A. One about _____

       B. Another about _____

  III. Made purchases

  IV. Two months later _____

2. <u>A successful job interview</u>   <u>depends on several factors.</u>
       subject   treatment

    I. Presenting good appearance

        A. _____

        B. _____

   II. Behaving properly

  III. Being qualified

        A. Education

        B. _____

  IV. Knowing something about the employer

3. <u>Joe's drug addiction</u>   <u>had significant effects on his life.</u>
       subject   treatment

    I. Developed mental-health problems

        A. _____

        B. _____

   II. Developed _____

  III. Lost his job

Exercise 6 Writing an Outline

Make a topic outline for your essay. Your Roman-numeral headings will probably correspond to some of the major divisions of your cluster.

✳ Writer's Guidelines at a Glance: Prewriting

1. The writing process consists of strategies that can help you produce a polished essay. **Prewriting** includes exploring, experimenting, gathering information, writing the controlling idea, and organizing and developing support. **Writing** includes drafting, revising, and editing.
2. Prewriting includes one or more of the following strategies.

   - **Freewriting:** writing without stopping so that you can explore, experiment, and invent

- **Brainstorming or listing:** responding to *Who? What? Where? When? Why?* and *How?* questions or making lists on likely divisions of your subject
- **Clustering:** showing related ideas by double-bubbling a subject and then connecting single bubbles of related ideas on spokes radiating out and branching from the hub
- **Composing the thesis:** writing a sentence that has two parts— the subject (what you are writing about) and the treatment (what you will do with the subject)
- **Outlining:** dividing the controlling idea into sections of support material, dividing those sections further, and establishing a workable sequence

✳ 4

The Writing Process:
Writing, Revising,
and Editing

✳ Writing Your First Draft

Once you have developed your thesis and your outline (or list or cluster), you are ready to begin writing your essay. The initial writing is called the **first, or rough, draft.** Your thesis statement is likely to be at or near the beginning of your essay and will be followed by your support as ordered by your outline.

Paying close attention to your outline for basic organization, you should proceed without worrying about the refinements of writing. This is not the time to concern yourself with perfect spelling, grammar, or punctuation. After you have finished that first draft, take a close look at it. If your thesis is sound and your outline has served you well, you now have a basic discussion. You have made a statement and supported it.

Don't be embarrassed by the roughness of your work. You should be embarrassed only if you leave it that way. You are seeing the reason why a first draft is called "rough." Famous authors have said publicly that they wouldn't show their rough drafts even to their closest, most forgiving friends.

The Recursive Factor

The process of writing can be called **recursive,** which means "going back and forth." In this respect, writing is like reading. If you do not understand what you have read, you back up and read it again. After you have read an entire passage, you may need to read it again selectively. The same can be said of writing. If, for example, after having developed an outline and started writing your first draft, you discover

52

that your subject is too broad, you will have to back up, narrow your thesis, and then adjust your outline. You may even want to return to an early cluster of ideas to see how you can use a smaller grouping of them. Revision is usually the most recursive of all parts of the writing process. You will go over your material again and again until you are satisfied that you have expressed yourself as well as you possibly can.

Your Audience

When you speak to a person, you routinely adjust what you say and how you say it. You should do the same for your audience when you write. To the extent that you can, consider the needs, interests, knowledge, and abilities of your intended readers and appropriately adjust your subject, explanations, style, and word choice.

✳ Revising Your Writing

The term *first draft* suggests quite accurately that there will be other drafts, or versions, of your writing. Only in the most dire situations, such as an in-class examination when you have time for only one draft, should you be satisfied with a single effort.

What you do beyond the first draft is revising and editing. Revising concerns itself with organization, content, and language effectiveness. Editing involves a final correcting of mistakes in spelling, punctuation, and capitalization. In practice, revising and editing are not always separate activities, although writers usually wait until the next-to-the-last draft to edit some minor details and attend to other small points that can be easily overlooked.

Successful revision almost always involves intense, systematic rewriting. You should learn to look for certain aspects of skillful writing as you enrich and repair your first draft. To help you recall these aspects so that you can keep them in mind and examine your material comprehensively, this textbook offers a memory device— an acronym in which each letter suggests an important feature of good writing and revision. This device enables you to memorize the features of good writing quickly. Soon you will be able to recall and refer to them automatically. These features need not be attended to individually when you revise your writing, although they may be. And they need not be attended to in the order presented here.

The acronym is CLUESS (pronounced "clues"), which provides this guide:

> *C*oherence
> *L*anguage
> *U*nity
> *E*mphasis
> *S*upport
> *S*entences

Coherence

Coherence is an orderly relationship of ideas, each leading smoothly and logically to the next. You must weave your ideas together so skillfully that the reader can easily see how one idea connects to another and to the central thought. This central thought, of course, is expressed in the topic sentence for a paragraph and in the thesis for an essay. You can achieve coherence efficiently by using an overall pattern, transitional words and expressions, repetition of key words and ideas, pronouns, and a consistent point of view.

Overall Pattern

Several chapters in this book discuss strategies for an overall plan, or pattern, of organization. Three basic patterns prevail: time (chronology), space, and emphasis (stress on ideas). Sometimes you will combine patterns. The coherence of each pattern can be strengthened by using transitional words such as these:

> Time: *first, then, soon, later, following, after, at that point*
> Space: *up, down, right, left, beyond, behind, above, below, before*
> Emphasis: *first, second, third, most, more*

Transitional Terms

Use transitional terms, conjunctive adverbs, to help your reader move easily from one idea to another. Each of the following sentences has one or more of these terms.

> *First* I realized I had to get a job to stay in school.
>
> *At the same time, however,* my track coach wanted the team to spend more hours working out.
>
> We were, *after all,* the defending champions.
>
> *Finally* I dropped one of my courses.

Other transitional terms include *moreover, in fact, nevertheless, then, thus, now, soon, therefore, consequently,* and *accordingly.*

Repetition of Key Words and Ideas

Repeat key words and phrases to keep the main subject in the reader's mind and to maintain the continuity necessary for a smooth flow of logical thought.

Pronouns

Pronouns, such as *this, that, those, he, her, them,* and *it,* provide natural connecting links in your writing. Why? Every pronoun refers to an earlier noun (called the **antecedent** of the pronoun) and thus carries the reader back to that earlier thought. Here are some examples:

> I tried to buy *tickets* for the concert, but *they* were all sold.
>
> Assertive *people* tend to make decisions quickly. However, *they* may not make the wisest decisions.

Language

In the revision process, the word *language* takes on a special meaning; it refers to usage, tone, and diction.

Usage

Usage is the kind or general style of language we use. All or almost all of us operate on the principle of appropriateness. If I used *ain't* as part of my explanations in this textbook, you would be surprised and probably disappointed. You would think about my word choice rather than about what I have to say. Why would you be surprised? Because *ain't* is not appropriate for my audience in this situation. If you write an essay containing slang, you will probably be understood, but if the slang is not appropriate, you will draw unfavorable attention to your words. That does not mean that slang does not have its place—it does. It can be imaginative and colorful. Often, though, it is only a weak substitute for more precise vocabulary.

Usage is an important part of writing and revising. Judge what is appropriate for your audience and your purpose. What kind of language is expected? What kind of language is best suited for accomplishing your purpose?

Tone

Have you ever heard someone say, "Don't talk to me in that tone of voice" or "I accepted what she was saying, but I didn't like the tone she used when she told me"? **Tone** in these contexts means that the sound of the speaker's voice and maybe the language choices conveyed disrespect to the listener. The tone could have represented any number of feelings about the subject matter and the audience. Tone can have as many variations as you can have feelings: it can, for example, be sarcastic, humorous, serious, cautionary, objective, groveling, angry, bitter, sentimental, enthusiastic, somber, outraged, or loving.

Let's say you are getting a haircut. Looking in those omnipresent mirrors bordered with pictures of people with different styles of haircuts, you see that the stylist is cutting off too much hair. You could use different tones in giving him or her some timely how-to instructions.

> *Objective, serious:* "If you don't mind, what I meant to say was that I would like a haircut proportioned just like that one there in the picture of Tom Cruise from *Rain Man.*"
>
> *Humorous:* "I hesitate to make suggestions to someone who is standing at my back and holding a sharp instrument near my throat, but I'm letting my hair grow out a bit, and I don't want you to take off a lot in the back and on the sides."
>
> *Angry and sarcastic:* "Look man, when I sat down, I said I wanted my hair cut in the design of Tom Cruise in *Rain Man.* The way you're hacking at it, you must've thought I said *Top Gun.*"
>
> *Conciliatory:* "I really like the way you cut my hair, and I can see that you are proportioning it with great care, but I would like my hair to be a bit longer than the style that I think you're working on. Do you remember how I used to get my hair cut about a year ago, a little longer on the sides and more bushy on top?"
>
> *Friendly:* "You came up with a great style that everyone liked. Could you give me one similar to that?"
>
> *Overbearing:* "Damn it, buddy. Will you watch what you're doing! I asked for a haircut, not a shave. If God had wanted me to have bare skin above my shoulders, he would've put the hair on my feet."

In speech, feelings and attitudes are represented by inflection, loudness, word choice, and language patterns. In writing, tone is conveyed mainly by word choice and order; it is closely related to style—the variations in the way you write, depending on your purpose. Your purpose is simply to present a particular idea in a particular context. The context implies the audience; it is important to use the tone appropriate for your audience.

Usually your tone will be consistent throughout your presentation, although for the informal essay often assigned in college, you may choose to begin in a lighthearted, amusing tone before switching to a more serious, objective mode.

Diction

Diction is word choice. If you use good diction, you are finding the best words for a particular purpose in addressing a certain audience. There is some overlap, therefore, between usage and diction.

The following list shows the difference between general and specific words.

General	Specific	More Specific
food	pastry	Twinkie
mess	grease	oil slicks on table
drink	soda	mug of root beer
odor	smell from grill	smell of frying onions

Another aspect of diction is freshness and originality of expression. To achieve those distinctions, you should avoid clichés, which are trite, familiar phrases. Consider this sentence:

> When the prince married Cinderella, her sisters went green with envy because she was now on easy street, leaving them out in the cold.

Those words were written by a person who doesn't care about communicating in a clear and interesting manner. It would be far better to say,

> When the prince married Cinderella, her sisters were envious because they had few prospects.

Here are some clichés to avoid:

young at heart	quick as a flash
rotten to the core	slow but sure
uphill battle	other side of the coin
more than meets the eye	breathless silence
bitter end	acid test
as luck would have it	better late than never
last but not least	six of one, half dozen of the other

These are ready-made expressions. A cliché master manipulates language as if it were a prefabricated building going up, not bothering to use any imagination and leaving little opportunity for his or her audience to use theirs. Good diction reflects the writer as an individual and is fresh, original, and clear.

Unity

A controlling idea, stated or implied, unifies every piece of good writing. It is the point around which the supporting material revolves. For a paragraph, the elements are the topic sentence and the supporting sentences. For an essay, the elements are the thesis and the supporting paragraphs. All the supporting material should be related to the topic sentence or the thesis.

Unity can be strengthened and made more apparent if you use a strong concluding statement at the end of the unit and if you repeat key words and phrases from time to time. A good check on unity is to ask yourself if everything in your paragraph or essay is subordinate to and derived from the controlling idea.

Don't confuse unity and coherence. Whereas coherence involves the clear movement of thought from sentence to sentence or paragraph to paragraph, unity means staying on the topic. A unified and coherent outline would become incoherent if the parts were scrambled, but the outline technically would still be unified. These qualities of writing go together. You should stay on the topic and make clear connections.

Emphasis

Emphasis, a feature of most good writing, helps the reader focus on the main ideas. It can be achieved in several ways but mainly through placement of key ideas and through repetition.

Placement of Ideas

The most emphatic part of any passage, whether a sentence or a book, is the last part, because we usually remember most easily what we read last. The second most emphatic part of a passage is the beginning, because our mind is relatively uncluttered when we read it. For these reasons, among others, the topic sentence or the thesis usually comes at the beginning of a piece, and it is often restated or reflected on at the end in an echoing statement.

Repetition of Key Words and Ideas

Repetition is one of the simplest devices in your writer's toolbox. The words repeated may be single words, phrases, slightly altered sentences, or synonyms. Repetition keeps the dominant subject in the reader's mind and maintains the continuity necessary for a smooth flow of logical thought.

You can use this valuable technique easily. If, as is done in the following example, you are discussing the effects of the school dropout problem, then the word *effect(s)*, along with synonyms such as *result(s)* or *consequence(s)*, and *school dropout(s)*, are likely to be repeated several times. Moreover, phrases giving insight into the issue may be repeated, perhaps with slight variation.

> The causes of the school dropout problem have received much attention recently, but the effects are just as important. One obvious result is that of unemployment or low-paying employment. The student who drops out of school is likely to be dropping into poverty, perhaps even into a lifelong condition. Another effect is juvenile crime. The young person who has no prospects for a good job and no hope all too frequently turns to illegal activities. A third result concerns the psychological well-being of the dropout. Although withdrawing from school seems to offer a quick, viable solution to perceived problems, it almost immediately has consequences for the dropout's self-esteem. Of course, these effects may also be tied to causes, such as drugs, poverty, crime, or psychological problems, but devastating repercussions are there at the far end of the causes-and-effects continuum, and youngsters who are contemplating dropping out should consider them with care.

A word of warning: The effective use of word and phrase repetition should not be confused with an irritating misuse of word repetition. We all at times get "hung up" on certain words, and the result is a negative response from our audience. Consider this awkward use of repetition:

> She looked at him and frowned. He returned the look and then looked away at a stranger looking for his lost keys.

That's too many *look*'s. Consider this version:

> She looked at him [*or, perhaps even better,* She frowned at him]. He glared back and then glanced away at a stranger searching for his lost keys.

The second version preserves the idea of people "looking" by using synonyms. It does not grate on the reader's mind as the first does.

Support

How much support does a piece of writing need? A good support paragraph fulfills its function by fully developing the topic sentence. An essay is complete when it fulfills its function of developing a thesis. Obviously, you will have to judge what is complete. With some subjects, you will need little supporting and explanatory material. With others, you will need much more. The points of support, in the form of examples, details, quotations, and explanations, should be placed in the best possible order. (See "Patterns of Support for the Thesis," p. 25, and "Support Paragraphs," p. 29, in Chapter 2 for more information.)

Sentences

In the revision process, the word *sentences* pertains to the variety of sentence patterns and the correctness of sentence structure.

Variety of Sentences

A passage that offers a variety of simple and complicated sentences satisfies the reader, just as a combination of simple and complicated foods go together in a good meal. The writer can introduce variety by including both short and long sentences, by using different sentence patterns, and by beginning sentences in different ways.

Length

In revising, examine your writing to make sure that sentences vary in length. A series of short sentences is likely to make the flow seem choppy and the thoughts disconnected. But single short sentences interspersed with longer ones often work very well. Because they are uncluttered with supporting points and qualifications, they often are direct and forceful. Consider using short sentences to emphasize points and to introduce ideas. Use longer sentences to provide details or show how ideas are related.

Variety of Sentence Patterns

Good writing includes a variety of sentence patterns. Although there is no limit to the number of sentences you can write, the conventional English sentence appears in only four basic patterns:

SIMPLE	She did the work well.
COMPOUND	She did the work well, and she was well paid.
COMPLEX	Because she did the work well, she was well paid.
COMPOUND-COMPLEX	Because she did the work well, she was well paid, and she was satisfied.

Each sentence pattern listed above has its own purposes and strengths. The simple sentence conveys a single idea. The compound sentence shows, by its structure, that two somewhat equal ideas are connected. The complex sentence shows that one idea is less important than another; that is, it is dependent on, or subordinate to, the idea in the main clause. The compound-complex sentence has the scope of both the compound sentence and the complex sentence.

Variety of Sentence Beginnings

Another way to provide sentence variety is to use different kinds of beginnings. A new beginning may or may not be accompanied by a changed sentence pattern. Among the most common beginnings, other than those starting with the subject of the main clause, are those that start with a prepositional phrase, a dependent clause, or a transitional connective (conjunctive adverb), such as *therefore, however,* or *in fact.*

- Prepositional phrase (in italics)

    In your fantasy, you are the star.

    Like casino owners, game show hosts want you to be cheery.

- Dependent clause (in italics)

    When the nighttime Wheel of Fortune *debuted,* the slot was occupied by magazine shows.

As Pat Sajak noted, viewers often solve the puzzle before the contestants do.

—*Lewis Grossberger,* "A Big Wheel"

- Transitional connective (in italics)

  Now you know.

  Therefore, you feel happy, excited, and a bit superior.

Problems with Sentences

A complete sentence must generally include an independent clause, which is a group of words that contains a subject and a verb and can stand alone. Some groups of words may sound interesting, but they are not correct sentences. Three common problem groupings are fragments, comma splices, and run-ons (see pp. 226–227 in Chapter 14, "Handbook").

- **Fragment:** A word grouping that is structurally incomplete is only a fragment of a sentence.

  Because he left. (This is a dependent clause, not a complete sentence.)

  Went to the library. (This has no subject.)

  She being the only person there. (This has no verb.)

  Waiting there for help. (This phrase has neither subject nor verb.)

  In the back seat under a book. (This phrase has two prepositional phrases but no subject or verb.)

- **Comma splice:** The comma splice consists of two independent clauses with only a comma between them.

  The weather was bad, we canceled the picnic. (A comma by itself cannot join two independent clauses.)

- **Run-on:** The run-on differs from the comma splice in only one way: it has no comma between the independent clauses.

  The weather was bad we canceled the picnic.

Fragments, comma splices, and run-ons can easily be fixed. You cannot fix them, however, until you can confidently identify them in your writing. Watch for them during the revision and editing stages of your writing.

If you frequently have problems with sentence structure and awkwardness of phrasing, be especially suspicious of long sentences.

Test each sentence of fifteen or more words for flaws. Try writing shorter, more direct sentences until you gain more confidence and competency. Then work with more sophisticated patterns.

✳ Adding Editing to Revision

Editing, the final stage of the writing process, involves a careful examination of your work. Look for problems with capitalization, omissions, punctuation, and spelling (COPS).

Before you submit your writing to your instructor, do what almost all professional writers do before sending their material along: read it aloud, to yourself or to a willing accomplice. Reading material aloud will help you catch any awkwardness of expression, omission and misplacement of words, and other problems that are easily overlooked by an author.

As you can see, writing is a process and is not a matter of just sitting down and "banging out" a statement. The parts of the process from prewriting to revising to editing are connected, and your movement is ultimately forward, but this process allows you to go back and forth in the recursive manner discussed earlier. If your outline is not working, perhaps the flaw is in your thesis. You may need to go back and fix it. If one section of your essay is skimpy, perhaps you will have to go back and reconsider the pertinent material in your outline or cluster. There you might find more details or alter your thesis so that you can move into more fertile areas of thought.

Let's return to Leah, whose work was shown in Chapters 2 and 3. After completing her first draft, Leah began revising, guided mainly by CLUESS:

Coherence	making one idea lead smoothly to the next
Language	ensuring proper usage, tone, and diction
Unity	using the thesis to unify the essay parts and the topic sentences to unify the developmental paragraphs
Emphasis	repeating words and phrases and placing of key parts at the beginning or end of units
Support	presenting evidence and reasoning in relation to the thesis and topic sentences
Sentences	using a variety of beginnings and patterns; avoiding fragments, comma splices, and run-ons

The following draft is neither Leah's first nor her last, but it is an early draft that shows her revision process. The draft also includes some editing (for *c*apitalization, *o*missions, *p*unctuation, and *s*pelling, or COPS). Her final draft is on pp. 20–22 in Chapter 2.

                    Razor Wire Sweat Lodge

                     My tribe is   twenty-one represented
            I am a Pomo Indian, one tribe of many

                                              always
            here on the prison grounds. I have had

                              Ancestors   in
     ⎡ tremendous interest in my Ancestry and their

     | customs, and the cultures of all Indian

     | tribes. The sacred sweat ceremonies, I've

     | cultural practices
Rewrite| found to be one of the most interesting. Many

     | other
     | women of all races here in the facility have

     | an   other benefits
     | also taken interest and found peace within

     ⎣ themselves from participating in the sweats.

        I want to discuss the prison sweat lodge,

        what we do in the preparation period, what we

        do when we're inside for the ceremony, and

        what we do afterwards.

                                 in our prison facility
            ⎡ The first step to sweating is the
Rewrite for |
stronger topic | preparation period. Before anyone can sweat
  sentence | concerning
            ⎣ there are many requirements, in what we wear/.

        how we are instructed (depending on how many

~~times we've gone)~~, and how we act.$_\wedge$ For ~~T~~wenty-
four hours before the sweat$_\wedge$ we fast.$_\wedge$ Participants should drink only ~~We can~~

Coherence

~~only drink~~ water or juices, but if someone

has health problems, we will excuse her. The

lava rocks have to$_\wedge$ heat in the fire approximately

three hours before we start sweating. The

Organize
Be more
concise

fire has to be built just right in a little

house shape.$_\wedge$ We put ~~Putting~~ all the rocks in the

middle with the wood standing like a teepee

around them; then the paper$_\wedge$ is stuffed between

and around the wood. Once there's a good fire

going$_\wedge$ we ~~start~~ tend to the sweat lodge

itself. Since we have no tarp to put on the

sweat lodge, the state has provided us with

plenty of blankets. The blankets have to cover

the s$_\wedge$eat lodge fully. We put at least three
     w

layers of blankets on the sweat lodge. We make

sure we leave about eight inches of blanket

around the bottom of the sweat lodge.$_\wedge$ By ~~Around~~

Coherence

this time some women have started making their

tobacco ties. These ties are used for sending ~~putting~~$_\wedge$

~~your~~ prayer on. We've ~~got to~~ [must] make sure the

sponsor is somewhere by the sweat lodge at all

times. ~~Also about~~ [As for] the rock [s,] we use thirty to

fifty of them [;] it depends on their size and how

many women are sweating that day. Then the

women are told to change into only muumuu[s]; the

state provides them also. Then we're read[y] to go

inside. The preparation period is very

important[, but] ~~and~~ everyone looks forward to it

being over.

Once everyone is inside the sweat lodge,

there are certain things [we] ~~you~~ must do. ~~The way~~

~~we enter is~~ first we enter counter clockwise[,]

and [once] inside we ~~maintain everything we do~~ [conduct all parts of the ceremony]

counter clockwise. There are four rounds in

the sweat[, each of] which lasts about twenty to thirty

minutes ~~each~~. We stress that no one [should] break our

circle inside the sweat lodge, but it ~~is~~ [sometimes happens.]

~~possible.~~ Some women can't handle the heat

inside we never make them stay. The praying

and singing is in the Sioux language since

Coherence [bracket]

Rephrase [bracket]

⌊our outside sponsor is Sioux. Not everyone

has to sing or pray. It's up to ~~them~~. As
                                    the individual.

someone finishes a prayer ~~they say for all~~
                          she mentions all her relatives

~~their relations~~, then the next person prays.

Agreement ⌈ Before ~~anyone even~~ enter*s* the sweat ~~they~~
                    we   *we*

have to make sure they have peace and

good feelings with all other members. The

tobacco ties hang over our heads in the

sweat or around our necks. (A̸lso) we take in

sage with us and smudge ourselves with it.
                                            for purification

After each round, new hot rocks are brought

Verb ⌈⌈ in. As these rocks are place*d* in the fire
tense

sweet grass is put on them. ~~All~~ we do inside
                            What

Be more
concise the sweat lodge is not only for ourselves,

but ~~for~~ our prayers for others. We maintain
       through

ourselves with humility during the whole

sweat.

When the sweat is over we enter the final

phase. We come out and throw our tobacco ties

in the fire pit. The ~~first thing~~ we ~~do is~~ hose
   to   *n*

ourselves down with plenty of cold water. The

refreshments are opened and someone goes after

food. Once we've eaten and changed our clothes∧

we start taking down the sweat. The blankets

have to be taken off the same way they were

carefully
put on and folded up∧~~good~~. The left-over wood

has to be put away and ~~on both~~ the blankets

must be covered
and the wood∧~~we put their covers~~. Any garbage

to
that's been left around is thrown in∧the

dumpster. Then we lock the gate and bid our

f
farewells until the next weekend. After it's

Move   *we*   *physically*
to end all over∧~~you really~~ feel ~~a sense of~~

ed
refresh∧~~ness~~, and clean~~liness~~∧ and peaceful~~ness~~.

Using the
Rewrite ~~The~~∧sweat lodge is a custom of most~~ly all~~

Indian tribes. Certain Indian tribes go about

from
it differently ~~than~~ others∧but once they're

all inside everyone feels of one whole being.

All three of the steps I've gone through are

Each week we
helpful for a successful sweat ceremony. ~~Many~~
∧
~~of us members~~ look forward to these

ceremonies ~~every week~~. They help us cope

better with the prison system.

Exercise 1 Revising and Editing a First Draft

Treat the following passage by Tara Newsome as your own rough draft and revise and edit it. First consider coherence, language, unity, emphasis, support, *and* sentences *(CLUESS). Then edit, correcting fundamentals such as* capitalization, omissions, punctuation, *and* spelling *(COPS).*

                              Quitting School

        Quitting school was not a big deal for me until I
realize all the effects of quitting would bring to my
life. At that time I didn't care. I plan to marry a few
months later after my high school graduation. I was happy
at the time.
        Quitting school was a big mistake because when I went
out to look for a job I couldn't qualify for any of the
good positions because of my lack of education. Instead I
took a job as in a fast-foods place where I had no future.
Then I went to work in a big company just doing simple
office work. When it came time for promotions I couldn't
pass the tests they gave. That was not all. As a result of
quitting school later. I couldn't even help my children
with their homework or buy the special things for them.
        I started my family when I was not even eighteen
years. The first year of my marriage was fine, then
things started to fall apart. My husband had quit school
too, and he didn't make much money, and as I mentioned, I
didn't make much either. We argued a lot mainly over
money. We couldn't get a big enough house for our family
so that we could have the privacy we needed. I quit work

to raise my kids and that when I really got in deep. My
car was getting old and money was not enough to make big
payments I had to buy another old car, which broke down
all the time. I started freaking out. The fighting got
worse and we had a divorce.

I was lucky that my parents decided to help me, and
now I am dedicated to getting a good education. I will
work hard to learn so me and my children can have a
better life.

✳ Writer's Guidelines at a Glance: Writing, Revising, and Editing

1. **Writing**
   Write your first draft, paying close attention to your outline or list or cluster. Do not concern yourself with perfect spelling, grammar, or punctuation.

2. **Revising (CLUESS)**

   <u>C</u>oherence

   - Are the ideas clearly related, each one to the others, and to the central idea?
   - Is there a clear pattern of organization (time, space, or emphasis)?
   - Is the pattern supported by words that suggest the basis of that organization (time: *now, then, later;* space: *above, below, up, down;* emphasis: *first, second, last*)?
   - Is coherence enhanced by the use of transitional terms, pronouns, repetition, and a consistent point of view?

   <u>L</u>anguage

   - Is the general style of language usage appropriate (properly standard and formal or informal) for the purpose of the piece and the intended audience?
   - Is the tone (language use showing attitude toward material and audience) appropriate?

- Is the word choice (diction) effective? Do the words convey precise meaning? Are they fresh and original?

Unity

- Are the thesis and every topic sentence clear and well stated? Do they indicate both subject and treatment?
- Are all points of support clearly related to and subordinate to the topic sentence of each paragraph and to the thesis of the essay?

Emphasis

- Are ideas properly placed (especially near the beginning and end) for emphasis?
- Are important words and phrases repeated for emphasis?

Support

- Is there adequate material—such as examples, details, quotations, and explanations—to support each topic sentence and the thesis?
- Are the points of support placed in the best possible order?

Sentence Structure

- Are the sentences varied in length and beginnings?
- Are the sentences varied in pattern (simple, compound, complex, and compound-complex)?
- Are all problems with sentence structure (fragments, comma splices, run-ons) corrected?

3. **Editing**

- Are all problems in such areas as *c*apitalization, *o*missions, *p*unctuation, and *s*pelling (COPS) corrected?

✳ 5

Descriptive Narration: Moving Through Time and Space

✳ A Natural Combination of Narration and Description

As patterns of writing, description and narration go together like macaroni and cheese. You would almost never describe something without relating it to something else, especially to a story or a narrative. And you would seldom narrate something (tell a story) without including some description. A narrative moves through time; a description moves mainly through space.

✳ The Narrative Pattern

In our everyday lives, we tell stories and invite other people to do so by asking questions such as "What happened at work today?" and "What did you do last weekend?" We are disappointed when the answer is "Nothing much." We may be equally disappointed when a person doesn't give us enough details or gives us too many and spoils the effect. After all, we are interested in people's stories and in the people who tell them. We like narratives.

What is a narrative? A **narrative** is an account of an incident or a series of incidents that make up a complete and significant action. A narrative can be as short as a joke, as long as a novel, or anything in between, including the essay. Each narrative has five properties.

Situation
Situation is the background for the action. The situation may be described only briefly, or it may even be implied. ("To celebrate my

72

seventeenth birthday, I went to the Department of Motor Vehicles to take my practical test for my driver's license.")

Conflict

Conflict is friction, such as a problem in the surroundings, with another person(s), or within the individual. The conflict, which is at the heart of each story, produces struggle. ("It was raining and my appointment was the last one of the day. The examiner was a serious, weary-looking man who reminded me of a bad boss I once had, and I was nervous.")

Struggle

Struggle, which need not be physical, is the manner of dealing with the conflict. The struggle adds action or engagement and generates the plot. ("After grinding on the ignition because the engine was already on, I had trouble finding the windshield wiper control. Next I forgot to signal until after I had pulled away from the curb. As we crept slowly down the rain-glazed street, the examiner told me to take the emergency brake off. All the while I listened to his pen scratching on his clipboard. 'Pull over and park,' he said solemnly.")

Outcome

Outcome is the result of the struggle. ("After I parked the car, the examiner told me to relax, and then he talked to me about school. When we continued, somehow I didn't make any errors, and I got my license.")

Meaning

Meaning is the significance of the story, which may be deeply philosophical or simple, stated or implied ("calmness promotes calmness").

These components are present in some way in all the many forms of the narrative. They are enhanced by the use of various devices such as the following:

- **Description** (the use of specific details to advance action, with images to make readers see, smell, taste, hear, and feel)

  the *rain-glazed street*

  listened to his *pen scratching*

- **Dialogue** (the exact words of the speakers, enclosed in quotation marks)

  "Pull over and park," he said solemnly.

- **Transitional words** (words, such as *after, finally, following, later, next, soon,* and *when,* that move a story forward, for narratives are usually presented in chronological order)

  Next I forgot to

  After I parked the car

Most narratives written as college assignments have an expository purpose (that is, they explain a specified idea). Often the narrative will be merely an extended example. Therefore, the meaning of the narrative is exceedingly important and should be clear, whether it is stated or implied.

✳ The Descriptive Pattern

Description is the use of words to represent the appearance or nature of something. Often called a **word picture,** description attempts to present its subject for the mind's eye. In doing so, it does not merely become an indifferent camera; instead, it selects details that will depict something well. Just what details the descriptive writer selects will depend on several factors, especially the type of description and the dominant impression in the passage.

Types of Description

On the basis of treatment of subject material, description is customarily divided into two types: objective and subjective.

Effective **objective description** presents the subject clearly and directly as it exists outside the realm of feelings. If you are explaining the function of the heart, the characteristics of a computer chip, or the renovation of a manufacturing facility, your description would probably feature specific, impersonal details. Most technical and scientific writing is objective in that sense. It is likely to be practical and utilitarian, making little use of speculation and poetic technique while focusing on details of sight.

Effective **subjective description** is also concerned with clarity and it may be direct, but it conveys a feeling about the subject and sets a mood while making a point. Because most expression involves personal views, even when it explains by analysis, subjective description (often called **emotional description**) has a broader range of uses than objective description.

Descriptive passages can have a combination of objective and subjective description; only the larger context of the passage will reveal the main intent.

Imagery

To convey your main concern effectively to readers, you will have to give some sensory impressions. These sensory impressions, collectively called **imagery,** refer to that which can be experienced by the senses—what we can see, smell, taste, hear, and touch.

Subjective description is more likely to use more images and words rich in associations than is objective description. But just as a fine line cannot always be drawn between the objective and the subjective, a fine line cannot always be drawn between word choice in one and in the other. However, we can say with certainty that whatever the type of description, careful word choice will always be important.

General and Specific Words

To move from the general to the specific is to move from the whole class or body to the individual(s); for example:

General	Specific	More Specific
food	pastry	Twinkie
mess	grease	oil slicks on table
drink	soda	mug of root beer
odor	smell from grill	smell of frying onions

Abstract and Concrete Words

Words are classified as abstract or concrete depending on what they refer to. **Abstract words** refer to qualities or ideas: *good, ordinary, ultimate, truth, beauty, maturity, love.* **Concrete words** refer to substances or things; they have reality: *onions, grease, buns, tables, food.* The specific concrete words, sometimes called **concrete particulars,** often support generalizations effectively and convince the reader of the accuracy of the account.

Dominant Impression

Never try to give all of the details in description; instead, be selective, picking only those that you need to make a dominant impression, always taking into account the knowledge and attitudes of your readers. Remember, description is not photographic. If you wish to describe a person, select only the traits that will project your intended dominant impression. If you wish to describe a landscape, do not give all the details that you might find in a picture; just pick the details that support what you want to say. That extremely important dominant impression is directly linked to your purpose and is created by the choosing and arranging of images, figurative language, and revealing details.

Useful Procedure for Writing Description

Description is seldom static. The framework usually includes some narrative pattern, as shown here.

> What is your subject? (school campus during summer vacation)
> What is the dominant impression? (deserted, reminding you of different times)
> What is the situation? (Note the natural entry of the narrative: You are walking across campus in early August.)
> What details support the dominant impression? (silence, dust on water fountain, bare bulletin boards)
> What is the movement (order) as you present details? (movement through time and space)

✳ Order for Descriptive Narration: Time and Space

All of the details of the descriptive narration must have some order, some sequence. Although the two patterns blend, time is the primary factor for telling a story, and space is the primary factor for describing an object or a scene. The following words will help you order time and space.

- Time: *first, second, then, soon, finally, while, after, next, later, now, before*
- Space: *next to, below, under, above, behind, in front of, beyond, in the foreground, in the background, to the left, to the right*

✳ Practicing Patterns of Descriptive Narration

Exercise 1 Completing Patterns

Fill in the blanks in the following outline to complete the descriptive narration.

Topic: last-minute shopping for a present

I. _____ (a certain department in a mall store)

   A. Other shoppers

      1. _____ (appearance)

      2. _____ (behavior)

   B. Condition and arrangement of merchandise (describe with appropriate details of imagery: sight, sound, taste, smell, and touch)

      1. _____

      2. _____

      3. _____

II. Can't find a particular item

   A. Search and search

   B. Start getting frustrated

   C. Meet an old friend (perhaps the person you are shopping for)

      1. _____ (description of friend)

      2. _____ (more description, perhaps adding person in action)

III. _____ (whatever the friend does to help)

   A. _____

   B. _____

IV. _____ (what you purchase or what you decide to do)

☀ Examining Essays of Descriptive Narration

Student Writer

My First Real Fire

Tyson M. Burns

Like many students at community colleges, Tyson M. Burns brings many life experiences with him. As a member of the National

Guard, he participated in Desert Shield (1990) and Desert Storm (1991), so his recent work as a firefighter was not his first taste of action. Here he narrates his real-life "baptism by fire."

Present tense throughout stresses immediacy

1   I am violently torn from my dream by the shrieking of the alarm. I am on autopilot, still half asleep and trying to

I. Situation

make my eyes focus as I jump into my boots and run for the fire engine. A mass of shoulders and elbows clash as we all put on our jackets and hoods. Somewhere above my head a loudspeaker comes to life, and the dispatcher tells us that the carpet warehouse down the street is fully engulfed in flames. My heart starts to race, and I feel a cold wave of adrenaline wash over my body.

2   The ride to the fire is a rough one. As I vigorously chew on a handful of Tums,

Concrete words

I steady myself by holding on to the <u>door handle</u> with my left hand and bring a <u>bottle of water</u> to my mouth with my right. I am trying to concentrate on what I will

Image: Sound

have to do when I get there. The <u>siren</u> and <u>air horns</u> are <u>deafening</u> as I run through the various procedures in my head. This is my first real fire. Will I get to go inside? What will it look like, feel like, and sound like inside? My Captain in the front seat looks back over his shoulder at

Dialogue	me and asks, "You want to get hot tonight?" I just nod my head as I adjust the straps on my facemask.
Concrete words	3 We are the first of four fire trucks to respond to the fire. We park on the street in front of the building. It is a typical <u>large plate glass storefront</u> with
Images: Sight	a <u>showroom in the front</u> and a <u>warehouse in the rear of the building</u>. <u>Thick black smoke</u> is billowing from the back of the building and rising in a huge <u>dark column</u>
Situation continued	that <u>blocks the stars</u>. I am assigned to a hose team and sandwiched between my Captain and Lieutenant. I am scared, but I feel much better going in with two experienced firefighters. In what seems like only a matter of seconds, the entry team cuts open one of the warehouse loading doors.
	4 As we crawl in, all I can see is the floor and my Captain's rear end. A
Image: Sound	<u>bubbling</u>, <u>sizzling</u>, <u>popping</u> sound fills my ears. I never thought I would hear frying bacon in a fire. The mechanical <u>clunk</u> and <u>hiss</u> of my breathing reminds me of Darth Vader from the old *Star Wars* movies. I am getting excited, and I have to remind myself to breathe slowly so that my air will last.

Image: Sight

5   When I look around, I see that I am surrounded by a thick cloud of bright orange light. I can only see about a foot and a half in front of me; my left hand is on the back of my Captain's air tank and our hose is in the crook of my right arm. Inside this swirling cloud, it looks like a hundred bright orange floodlights are shining down on us from all directions. I

Image: Touch

feel the hose jerk and then vibrate as my Captain opens the nozzle at the end of the hose and sprays water over our heads. I wait for a few seconds. When I do not feel boiling hot water come back down on

II. Conflict

us, I know we are in trouble.

6   The heat is intense. It must be over 500 degrees in here. It almost takes my

III. Struggle

breath away, like when you first enter a steam room and you catch your breath. In those first few seconds, you have a slight

**Images:
Touch**

panic; your skin burns and your face stings. But after a few moments you get used to it and realize you are okay. Before I know it, I am sweating profusely, but instead of it cooling me I can feel it heat up and begin to burn my skin. The

Image: Smell

cool stale air that I had been breathing is now getting warmer and smelling like

Image: Touch

plastic as my air tank begins to heat up. The rubber around my facemask is getting hotter and beginning to <u>sting my face</u>. I wonder how much heat my protective equipment can take. I wonder how much more I can take. I do not want to disappoint my Captain and Lieutenant.

Image: Sound   7

Image: Touch

I hear a <u>muffled, garbled yelling</u> behind me and <u>feel a hand slapping my left shoulder</u>. I arch my back and turn my head so that I can hear my Lieutenant better. Through his mask I hear him <u>yell</u>, "IT'S

Dialogue

Image: Sound

TOO HOT, IT'S GONNA FLASH OVER, WE NEED TO GET THE HECK OUTTA HERE!!" I relay the message to my Captain, and he agrees. I feel him get up from his knees to a crouch and head for the doorway. I follow him, my left hand never leaving his air tank. As

IV. Outcome

Image: Touch

we emerge from the opening, I <u>feel</u> my Lieutenant <u>slam</u> into the back of me, knocking us all down like dominoes. I roll off my Captain and look up at what should have been a smoke-filled sky. Instead, I

Image: Sight

see <u>bright orange flames rolling</u> over our heads from the doorway we had just come

Image: Touch

through. A second later I <u>feel</u> invisible <u>hands grabbing</u> my harness and <u>dragging</u> me across the parking lot.

8	My helmet and mask are jerked off my
Image: Touch	head. I feel the night air instantly cool
	my cheeks and sweat-soaked hair. A voice
Dialogue	asks, "Can you tell me what your name is?
	Do you know where you are right now?" I
	look down to see if all of my body parts
	are still attached, and I notice that my
Image: Sight	whole body is smoking, as if steam is
	escaping through the fabric of my coat and
	pants. My Lieutenant was right. The flames
	must have flashed over as we were exiting.
	The paramedic who is checking me out
	notices that I am staring at my steaming
Dialogue	gloves and says, "You guys were just
	coming through the doorway as it spewed
	this huge ball of fire. Just like when
	circus performers spit mouthfuls of
	alcohol across a match." As I throw up,
	the other firefighters are laughing and
	patting me on the back and saying, "So,
	how does it feel to be a real
V. Meaning	firefighter?"
9	Fabulous.

Professional Writer

The Jacket

Gary Soto

Gary Soto was born in Fresno, California, in 1952 to working-class Mexican-American parents. In his youth he worked in the neighborhood and in nearby fields. Later he would discover his talent for writing, attend Fresno City College and California State University at Fresno, and become a prominent author of poetry, short stories, essays, and novels. His books include Living Up the Street, Nickel and Dime, Taking Sides, *and* Baseball in April and Other Stories.

1   My clothes have failed me. I remember the green coat that I wore in fifth and sixth grades when you either danced like a champ or pressed yourself against a greasy wall, bitter as a penny toward the happy couples.

2   When I needed a new jacket and my mother asked what kind I wanted, I described something like bikers wear: black leather and silver studs with enough belts to hold down a small town. We were in the kitchen, steam on the windows from her cooking. She listened so long while stirring dinner that I thought she understood for sure the kind I wanted. The next day when I got home from school, I discovered draped on my bedpost a jacket the color of day-old guacamole. I threw my books on the bed and approached the jacket slowly, as if it were a stranger whose hand I had to shake. I touched the vinyl sleeve, the collar, and peeked at the mustard-colored lining.

3   From the kitchen Mother yelled that my jacket was in the closet. I closed the door to her voice and pulled at the rack of clothes in the closet, hoping the jacket on the bedpost wasn't for me but my mean brother. No luck. I gave up. From my bed, I stared at the jacket. I wanted to cry because it was so ugly and so big that I knew I'd have to wear it a long time. I was a small kid, thin as a young tree, and it would be years before I'd have a new one. I stared at the jacket, like an enemy, thinking bad things before I took off my old jacket whose sleeves climbed halfway to my elbow.

4   I put the big jacket on. I zipped it up and down several times, and rolled the cuffs up so they didn't cover my hands. I put my hands in the pockets and flapped the jacket like a bird's wings. I stood in front of the mirror, full face, then profile, and then looked over my shoulder as if someone had called me. I sat on the bed, stood against the bed, and combed my hair to see what I would look like doing something natural. I looked ugly. I threw it on my brother's bed and looked at it for a long time before I slipped it on and went out to the backyard, smiling a "thank you" to my mom as I passed her in the kitchen. With my hands in my pockets I kicked a ball against the

fence, and then climbed it to sit looking into the alley. I hurled orange peels at the mouth of an open garbage can and when the peels were gone I watched the white puffs of my breath thin to nothing.

5   I jumped down, hands in my pockets, and in the backyard on my knees I teased my dog, Brownie, by swooping my arms while making bird calls. He jumped at me and missed. He jumped again and again, until a tooth sunk deep, ripping an L-shaped tear on my left sleeve. I pushed Brownie away to study the tear as I would a cut on my arm. There was no blood, only a few loose pieces of fuzz. Damn dog, I thought, and pushed him away hard when he tried to bite again. I got up from my knees and went to my bedroom to sit with my jacket on my lap, with the lights out.

6   That was the first afternoon with my new jacket. The next day I wore it to sixth grade and got a D on a math quiz. During the morning recess Frankie T., the playground terrorist, pushed me to the ground and told me to stay there until recess was over. My best friend, Steve Negrete, ate an apple while looking at me, and the girls turned away to whisper on the monkey bars. The teachers were no help: They looked my way and talked about how foolish I looked in my new jacket. I saw their heads bob with laughter, their hands half-covering their mouths.

7   Even though it was cold, I took off the jacket during lunch and played kickball in a thin shirt, my arms feeling like braille from goose bumps. But when I returned to class I slipped the jacket on and shivered until I was warm. I sat on my hands, heating them up, while my teeth chattered like a cup of crooked dice. Finally warm, I slid out of the jacket but a few minutes later put it back on when the fire bell rang. We paraded out into the yard where we, the sixth graders, walked past all the other grades to stand against the back fence. Everybody saw me. Although they didn't say out loud, "Man, that's ugly," I heard the buzz-buzz of gossip and even laughter that I knew was meant for me.

8   And so I went, in my guacamole jacket. So embarrassed, so hurt, I couldn't even do my homework. I received Cs on quizzes, and forgot the state capitals and the rivers of South America, our friendly neighbor. Even the girls who had been friendly blew away like loose flowers to follow the boys in neat jackets.

9   I wore that thing for three years until the sleeves grew short and my forearms stuck out like the necks of turtles. All during

that time no love came to me—no little dark girl in a Sunday dress she wore on Monday. At lunchtime I stayed with the ugly boys who leaned against the chainlink fence and looked around with propellers of grass spinning in our mouths. We saw girls walk by alone, saw couples, hand in hand, their heads like bookends pressing air together. We saw them and spun our propellers so fast our faces were blurs.

10   I blame that jacket for those bad years. I blame my mother for her bad taste and her cheap ways. It was a sad time for the heart. With a friend I spent my sixth-grade year in a tree in the alley waiting for something good to happen to me in that jacket, which had become the ugly brother who tagged along wherever I went. And it was about that time that I began to grow. My chest puffed up with muscle and, strangely, a few more ribs. Even my hands, those fleshy hammers, showed bravely through the cuffs, the fingers already hardening for the coming fights. But that L-shaped rip on the left sleeve got bigger; bits of stuffing coughed out from its wound after a hard day of play. I finally Scotch-taped it closed, but in rain or cold weather the tape peeled off like a scab and more stuffing fell out until that sleeve shriveled into a palsied arm. That winter the elbows began to crack and whole chunks of green began to fall off. I showed the cracks to my mother, who always seemed to be at the stove with steamed-up glasses, and she said that there were children in Mexico who would love that jacket. I told her that this was America and yelled that Debbie, my sister, didn't have a jacket like mine. I ran outside, ready to cry, and climbed the tree by the alley to think bad thoughts and watch my breath puff white and disappear.

11   But whole pieces still casually flew off my jacket when I played hard, read quietly, or took vicious spelling tests at school. When it became so spotted that my brother began to call me "camouflage," I flung it over the fence into the alley. Later, however, I swiped the jacket off the ground and went inside to drape it across my lap and mope.

12   I was called to dinner: Steam silvered my mother's glasses as she said grace; my brother and sister with their heads bowed made ugly faces at their glasses of powered milk. I gagged too, but eagerly ate big rips of buttered tortilla that held scooped up beans. Finished, I went outside with my jacket across my arm. It was a cold sky. The faces of clouds were piled up, hurting. I climbed the fence, jumping down with a grunt. I started up the

alley and soon slipped into my jacket, that green ugly brother who breathed over my shoulder that day and ever since.

Exercise 2 Discussion and Critical Thinking

1. Why is the jacket more of a disappointment than it would have been if Soto's mother had given it to him as a surprise?

2. What kind of jacket did Soto request?

3. How is the jacket like a person and an evil force?

4. What are some of the failures Soto attributes to his jacket?

5. Why doesn't he lose it or throw it away?

✳ Topics for Essays of Descriptive Narration

Reading-Related and Text-Based Topics

For text-based writing, use references to and quotations from the reading.

"My First Real Fire"

1. Using this essay as a model, write about your being initiated at the workplace through a scary or threatening experience. The job might involve working with potentially dangerous equipment, dealing with elements (fire, water, air, or land), or mixing with intimidating, obnoxious, or creepy people.

"The Jacket"

2. Frequently reprinted, this essay is enormously popular with student readers. Discuss the likely reasons for its popularity. Refer directly to the essay and use quotations in your discussion.

3. Write about an embarrassing article of clothing you wore as a child, an article that you thought at the time had an influence on how others felt about you and certainly how you felt about yourself.

4. Write about an article of clothing you wore with pride as a child or one that you now wear with pride.

5. Use your imagination to write about the jacket from the mother's point of view. You might also imagine that she is providing her viewpoint just after reading this essay by her son; therefore, she can refer to what Gary Soto said.

6. Write about the jacket from the jacket's point of view. Refer to particular incidents in the essay. Use references to the essay and quotes from it.

Cross-Curricular Topics

7. Use description in the following assignments.

- Agriculture: Field-trip report
- Art History: Report on a museum or a particular work of art
- Education: School-visit report
- Ecology: Field-trip report
- Geology: Field-trip report
- Sociology: Report on a field trip to an urban zone, a prison, or another institution

Career-Related Topics

8. Write a descriptive narration about an event at work that was exceedingly satisfying or unsatisfying.

9. Describe a person performing a job in a stressful situation. Point out what the person did that was right and wrong.

10. Write about your best or worst moment searching for a job, being interviewed for a job, or training for a job. Focus on a brief period of time so that you can include descriptive detail.

General Topics

Write a descriptive narration about one of the following subjects. Limit the time frame so that you can include descriptive detail.

11. A ceremony such as a graduation, funeral, or wedding

12. A time when you made a proposal of marriage (or received one) or applied for a position you wanted

13. A time when you confronted authority or had to deliver bad news

14. Your first date, first day in a new school, first public performance, first time in love

15. The time you met (saw) a most impressive doctor, teacher, speaker, singer, irritating person, salesperson, or police officer

16. The occasion when you witnessed an accident or a natural disaster such as a tornado or flood

✳ Writer's Guidelines at a Glance: Descriptive Narration

Narration

1. Include the following points to be sure you have a complete narration:

   Situation
   Conflict
   Struggle
   Outcome
   Meaning

2. Consider using dialogue.
3. Give details concerning action.

Description

1. In an objective description, use direct, practical language and appeal mainly to the sense of sight.
2. In an emotional description, appeal to the reader's feelings, especially through images of sight, sound, smell, taste, and touch.
3. Use specific and concrete words if appropriate.
4. Relate your details to the dominant impression of your description.

Descriptive Narration

1. All of your details must have an order or a sequence. Although the two patterns blend, time is the primary factor for telling a story, whereas space is the primary factor for description.

   - Words indicating time include *first, second, then, soon, finally, while, after, next, later, now,* and *before.*
   - Words indicating space include *next to, below, under, above, behind, in front of, beyond, in the foreground, in the background, to the left,* and *to the right.*

2. Both description and narration in college writing usually have an expository purpose; that is, they explain a specified or implied idea.

✳ 6

Exemplification: Writing with Examples

✳ Writing Essays of Exemplification

Exemplification means using examples to explain, convince, or amuse. Lending interest and information to writing, exemplification is one of the most common and effective ways of developing ideas. Examples may be developed in as much as a paragraph or more, or they may be phrases or only single words, as in the following sentence: "Children like packaged breakfast foods, such as *Wheaties, Cheerios,* and *Rice Krispies.*"

Characteristics of Good Examples

As supporting information, the best examples are vivid, specific, and representative. These three qualities are closely linked; collectively, they must support the topic sentence of a paragraph and the thesis of the essay. The **vivid** example attracts attention. Through a memorable presentation and the use of identifying names, the example becomes **specific** to the reader. A good example must also be **representative;** that is, it must be experienced as typical so that it can be the basis for a generalization.

Finally, and most important, the connection between the example and the thesis must be clear. A bizarre case of cheating may be fascinating in itself (vivid and specific), but in an essay on "the hard work of cheating," that example must also support (represent) the thesis. The reader should say, in effect, "That's interesting, convincing, and memorable. Though it's unusual, I can see that it's typical of what goes on."

Techniques for Finding Examples

Writing a good essay of exemplification begins, as always, with prewriting. The techniques you use will depend on what you are writing about. Assuming that you begin with a topic idea, one useful technique is listing. Base your list on what you have read, heard, and experienced. Here is a list on the topic "the hard work of cheating":

> The two times when I cheated: copied homework, brought in list for a biology test, felt guilty
> A person who bought a research paper
> Jess, who copied from me
> The Internet "Cheaters" source
> The two persons who exchanged identities
> More work than it's worth
> More stress than it's worth

✳ Practicing Patterns of Exemplification

Exercise 1 Completing Patterns

Fill in the blanks in the following outlines to add more examples that support the thesis.

1. Thesis: Some people let television watching interfere with their social lives.

    I. Watching football games at a family gathering on holidays

    II. Watching television in a _____

    III. _____

2. Thesis: Most successful movies are more concerned with action than character, and the action is violent.

    I. (Name of movie) _____

    II. (Name of movie) _____

    III. (Name of movie) _____

✳ Examining Essays of Exemplification

Student Writer

Hungering for Sounds of Silence
Eileen Baylor

The assignment for student Eileen Baylor was to select an article from a list and write a brief essay of reaction to it. She was to convey the important ideas of her subject piece with direct references and quotations, but she was not to feature a summary of it. She was required to photocopy the article; underline and annotate it; and submit it along with a brief outline, a rough draft, and a typed final draft of her brief essay of reaction.

1 "Cell Phone Backlash" by Margaret Loftus is full of good examples. They are good because they support her main point and remind me of similar examples. Like many people, Loftus is sick and tired of loud secondhand cell phone talking.

2 The worst part is that the offensive, loud talking is getting worse. She says, "Nearly 75 percent of those surveyed in our poll think mobile phone etiquette has declined over the past five years" (26). One may be inclined to distrust an "our poll," but Loftus backs hers up by referring to a National Geographic Traveler/Yahoo! poll concluding that 75 percent of travelers are "sometimes or frequently annoyed" (26). For airline travelers, that percentage may go up because the Federal Communications Commission may allow companies to remove its ban on cell phone use during flights.

3   Some of those who are already annoyed
are very annoyed. Loftus gives several
colorful examples. One is about a
loudmouth traveler calling numerous friends
to brag about where he was staying, where
he was dining, and which limousine service
he had booked. For revenge, an annoyed
fellow traveler slipped outside and used
his own cell phone to cancel all the

Example   reservations. In another example, a man on
a commuter train finally had had enough of
a long secondhand conversation about a
fellow passenger's divorce, including
custody of the dog. Finally he walked
across the aisle, grabbed the phone, and
smashed it on the floor of the train. In
still another example, a person confessed
he carries an illegal "jammer that kills
cell phone conversations within a 20-foot
radius" (26).

Topic   4   <u>Stories like that</u> may be satisfying to
sentence
Transition   those of us who are irritated by the
noise, but those solutions are not good
ideas for the general public. Canceling
the reservations may be just punishment,
but it is the kind of punishment that can
lead to retaliation. Smashing the cell
phone invites a violent response. And not

only is jamming the phone illegal, as
mentioned, but it might prevent a call
coming through about a medical
emergency.

Topic sentence 5 <u>Those reservations do not mean I am
pure of thought</u>. I have concocted my own
unwholesome schemes during loud cell phone
conversations at restaurants, in shopping
lines, and even one in a church at a
Extended example funeral. Last week in a restaurant a
nearby loudmouth had a cell phone
conversation with his wife about her
purchasing a tablecloth. He told her the
one she was considering was too expensive
and that she should shop for a cheaper one
on the Web. He even told his wife he was
dining alone, though a sweet young thing
sat smiling across from him. I will admit
I thought up a plot of how I could blow
his cover, but instead I just left without
ordering dessert.

Topic sentence Transition 6 <u>In another incident</u> I witnessed in a
<u>middle-scale restaurant, a man came in
alone and sat in a booth across from me.</u>
Extended example Almost immediately I heard static, electric
ratchet wrench sounds, and booming voices.
He had brought a walkie-talkie with him
and was monitoring calls from his nearby

place of work in a large tire store. He
was a huge man, mean-looking and sweaty.
He could carry a tire in either hand--
above his head. I stared at him. He glared
back. I thought of suggesting he use his
cell phone. Politely.

7   Right then I concluded that Loftus was
right in her article about cell phone
etiquette. Things are bad and getting
worse, but maybe she does not know what
worse is. Maybe cell phones are just a
threshold weapon in rudeness. I ordered a
dessert to go.

Work Cited

Loftus, Margaret. "Cell Phone Backlash."

National Geographic Traveler July/
August 2005:26.

Professional Writer

Who's Cheap?

Adair Lara

Adair Lara is an award-winning newspaper columnist for the San
Francisco Chronicle *and the author of five books and dozens of
magazine articles. Her best-selling memoir about raising a teenage
daughter,* Hold Me Close, Let Me Go, *was published by Random
House (2001). Her specialty is writing about her experiences in
first-person point of view.*

1   It was our second date, and we had driven one hundred miles
up the coast in my car to go abalone-diving. When I stopped to
fill the tank at the only gas station in sight, Craig scowled and
said, "You shouldn't get gas here. It's a rip-off."

2   But he didn't offer to help pay. And that night, after dinner in a restaurant, he leaned over and whispered intimately, "You get the next one." Though he was sensitive and smart, and looked unnervingly good, Craig was as cheap as a two-dollar watch.

3   This is not an ethical dilemma, you're all shouting. *Lose the guy*, and fast.

4   Lose the guy? Is this fair? My friend Jill is always heading for the john when the check comes, but I don't hear anybody telling me to lose *her*. And she's far from the only cheap woman I know. A lot of us make decent money these days, yet I haven't seen women knocking over tables in fights for the lunch tab. In fact, many women with 20/20 vision seem to have trouble distinguishing the check from the salt, pepper and other tabletop items. But if a guy forgets to chip in for gas or gloats too long over the deal he got on his Nikes, he's had it.

5   Why is this double standard so enduring? One reason is that, while neither sex has a monopoly on imperfection, there *are* such things as flaws that are much more distasteful in one sex than in the other. Women seem especially unpleasant when they get drunk, swear or even insist on pursuing an argument they'll never win. And men seem beneath contempt when they're cheap.

6   These judgments are a holdover from the days when women stayed home and men earned the money. Though that old order has passed, we still associate men with paying for things. And besides, there's just something appealing about generosity. Buying something for someone is, in a sense, taking care of her. The gesture says, "I like you, I want to give you something." If it comes from a man to whom we are about to entrust our hearts, this is a comforting message. We miss it when it's not forthcoming.

7   Then why *not* dump on cheap men?

8   Some men are just skinflints and that's it. My friend Skye broke up with her boyfriend because when they went to the movies he doled out M&M's to her one at a time. Craig, my date back at the gas station, liked to talk about how he'd bought his car—which in California, where I live, is like buying shoes—as a special present to himself.

9   This kind of cheapness is ingrained; you'll never change it. That guy who parks two miles away to avoid the parking lot fee was once a little boy who saved his birthday money without being told to. Now he's a man who studies the menu and sputters, "Ten dollars for *pasta?*" His stinginess will always grate on

you, since he is likely to dole out his feelings as parsimoniously as his dollars.

10   On the other hand, I know a wonderful man, crippled with debts from a former marriage, who had to break up with a woman because she never paid her share, and he was simply running out of money. Though she earned a lot more than he did, she couldn't expand her definition of masculinity to include "sometimes needs to go Dutch treat."

11   To men, such women seem grasping. One friend of mine, who spends a lot of money on concerts and theater and sailing but not on restaurants he considers overpriced, has evolved a strategy for women who are annoyed at the bohemian places he favors. If his date complains, he offers to donate to the charity of her choice the cost of an evening at her favorite spot. "Some women have bad values," he says, "And if the idea of spending money on a good cause, but not on her, makes her livid, I know she's one of them."

12   I had a bracing encounter with my own values when I told my friend Danny the humorous (I thought) story of a recent date who asked if I wanted a drink after a concert, then led me to the nearest water fountain.

13   Danny gave one of his wry looks. "Let's get this straight," he said, laughing. "As a woman, you are so genetically precious that you deserve attention just because you grace the planet. So, of course, he should buy you drinks. He should also drive the car, open the door, ask you to dance, coax you to bed. And then when you feel properly pampered, you can let out that little whine about how he doesn't treat you as an equal."

14   On second thought, I guess I'd rather buy my own drink.

15   So here's the deal. Before dumping a guy for ordering the sundowner dinner or the house white, better first make sure that you aren't burdening the relationship with outdated ideas of how the sexes should behave. Speaking for myself, I know that if a man looks up from the check and says, "Your share is eleven dollars," part of me remembers that, according to my mother, *my* share was to look charming in my flowered blouse.

16   Wanting the man to pay dies hard. What many of us do now is *offer* to split the check, then let our purses continue to dangle from the chair as we give him time to realize that the only proper response is to whip out his own wallet.

17   Is this a game worth playing? It's up to you, but consider

that offering to help pay implies that the check is his responsibility. And this attitude can work both ways. My sister gets angry when her husband offers to help clean the house. "Like it's *my* house!" she snorts.

18   Like it's *his* check.

Exercise 2 Discussion and Critical Thinking

1. Lara uses examples to explain how she came to a conclusion on who—male, female, or both—should pay on dates. What does she think about the occasion of her second date with Craig when he does not pay for the gas or meal?

2. What examples does she use to show that some men are just "skinflints"?

3. In your estimation, who is worse on the 1–10 cheapness scale, the one-at-a-time M&M guy or the water-fountain guy?

4. In paragraph 9, Lara says that some men have ingrained cheapness and that men who are stingy with money are likely to be stingy with feelings. She offers no other support. Do you agree with her generalization? Why or why not?

5. The author seems impressed by the man (in paragraph 11) who says he takes dates to inexpensive restaurants and if they complain, he offers to give the money he saved to a worthy cause of his date's choice. If she does not accept, he assumes she is just interested in having the fine meal for herself. Do you think that is likely a good way to discover his date's value system (as he believes), or is it likely that he has just devised a good way to avoid paying more?

6. What paragraph carries Lara's conclusion on her main question?

✳ Topics for Essays of Exemplification

Reading-Related and Text-Based Topics

"Hungering for Sounds of Silence"

1. Write a paragraph or an essay in which you disagree or agree with the main view expressed in this essay. Use some of your own examples from personal experience. If you think Baylor's view is an overreaction, explain why it is. Does age or generation have anything to do with how an individual is likely to react to secondhand cell phone conversations?

"Who's Cheap?"

2. Write a text-based essay in which you address some of the questions in Exercise 2. Agree or disagree with Adair Lara, as you examine her use of numerous examples leading to her conclusion that from now on she will pay her part of the check. Keep in mind that at the end of her essay, she knows what she'll say after the meal. She'll say, "I'll pay half," not "Let me pay half." Discuss the difference and whether it matters from your male or female perspective. Consider using some examples from your own experience.

3. In a broader sense, do you believe that one person is obliged to pay for the expenses of the date? If so, who should pay? Should the person who asked for the date pay? What if the female of a heterosexual couple asked for the date? Try to incorporate some ideas from Lara's essay into your own.

Cross-Curricular Topics

4. Use examples as supporting information in discussing a person, an event, or an issue pertaining to another class you have taken or are taking. Your explanation might focus on why someone or something was successful or unsuccessful. As a report on a field trip, examples might support a dominant impression of, say, a museum exhibit, in an art-history class, or an observation for a case study in an education or a psychology class.

Career-Related Topics

Use specific examples to support one of the following statements as applied to business, work, or career preparation.

5. My chosen career field requires much preparation.
6. If I had been the boss at the place where I worked, I would have handled certain situations differently.
7. "Burning bridges" should be done in warfare, not in work situations.
8. In some places where I worked [or went to school], sexual harassment occurred on an almost daily basis.
9. Sometimes one does a lot of tongue-biting and pride-swallowing when dealing with irate customers.
10. The women managers I know have really had to prove their competency.

General Topics

Develop an essay mainly by using examples to support one of these thesis statements.

11. We are surrounded by people with bad manners.
12. Most of what I really like is bad for me or someone else.
13. I am trying to live with certain problems I can't solve.
14. Some of our modern conveniences are causing some of our biggest problems.
15. One can tell much about people by the way they eat [or dress, talk, react to stressful situations, relate to their family and friends].
16. I would be happier if I could divorce some of my relatives.
17. Some people who think they are nonconformists are conforming to their own group.
18. College [or staying at home, working full-time, having a large family, getting married] is not for everyone.

☀ Writer's Guidelines at a Glance: Exemplification

1. Use examples to explain, convince, or amuse.
2. Use examples that are vivid, specific, and representative.

   - Vivid examples attract attention.
   - Specific examples are identifiable.
   - Representative examples are typical and therefore the basis for generalization.

3. Tie your examples clearly to your thesis.
4. Draw your examples from what you have read, heard, and experienced.
5. Brainstorm a list of possible examples before you write.

7

Analysis by Division:
Examining the Parts

✳ Writing Essays of Analysis by Division

If you need to explain how something works or exists as a unit, you will write an analysis by division. You will break down a unit (your subject) into its parts and explain how each part functions in relation to the operation or existence of the whole. The most important word here is *unit*. You begin with something that can stand alone or can be regarded separately: a poem, a heart, a painting, a car, a bike, a person, a school, a committee.

The following procedure will guide you in writing an analysis by division: Move from subject to principle, to division, to relationship.

Step 1: Begin with something that is a unit (subject).
Step 2: State one principle by which the unit can function.
Step 3: Divide the unit into parts according to that principle.
Step 4: Discuss each of the parts in relation to the unit.

You might apply that procedure to writing about a good boss in the following way:

1. Unit — Manager
2. Principle of function — Effective as a leader
3. Parts based on the principle — Fair, intelligent, stable, competent in the field
4. Relationship of parts to the unit — Consider each part in relation to the person's effectiveness as a manager.

Organization

In an essay of analysis by division, the main parts are likely to be the main points of your outline or main extensions of your cluster.

If they are anything else, reconsider your organization. A basic outline of an analysis by division might look like this:

> *Thesis:* To be effective as a leader, a manager needs specific qualities.
>
>   I. Fairness
>   II. Intelligence
>   III. Stability
>   IV. Competence in the field

Sequence of Parts

The order in which you discuss the parts will vary according to the nature of the unit and the way in which you view it. Here are some possible sequences for organizing the parts of a unit:

- **Time:** The sequence of the parts in your paragraph or essay can be mainly chronological, or time-based (if you are dealing with something that functions on its own, such as a heart, with the parts presented in relation to stages of the function).
- **Space:** If your unit is a visual object, especially if, like a pencil, it does nothing by itself, you may discuss the parts in relation to space. In the example of the pencil, the parts of the pencil begin at the top with the eraser and end at the bottom with the pencil point.
- **Emphasis:** Because the most emphatic location of any piece of writing is the end (the second most emphatic point is the beginning), consider placing the most significant part of the unit at the end.

Two Uses of Analysis by Division

From the wide range of uses of analysis by division mentioned in the introduction, two are featured in this chapter: the restaurant review and the short story review.

Restaurant Review

Definition

The **restaurant review** is an article of one or more paragraphs that describes three elements: ambiance, service, and food.

- **Ambiance** is the atmosphere, mood, or feeling of a place. For restaurants, it may begin with landscaping and architecture (building style). Ambiance is certainly produced by what is inside, such as the furnishings, seating, style, upkeep, sounds, sights, smells, behavior of other customers, and management style—whatever produces that mood or the feeling, even if it is franchise plastic and elevator music.

- **Service** is mainly concerned with food delivery and those who do it: their attitude, manners, helpfulness, promptness, accuracy, and availability. Self-service or pickup establishments would be judged by similar standards.
- **Food** is the emphasis—its variety, quality, quantity, price, and presentation.

Writing the Review

- Use first person (*I*) as you relate your experience in a particular restaurant or chain.
- If possible, base your evaluation on more than one item. Here is a low-cost way to do that: Dine with others and ask your companions to order different foods. Then ask them if you can taste (two small bites will suffice) what they are served, thus increasing your experience. Offering to pay a portion of their check may make others more receptive to sharing their food.
- While you are dining, use a simple outline or listing to make sure you have information on ambiance, service, and food. Copy names of foods and prices from the menu. Use quotation marks around any descriptive phrases for items you copy.
- You need not separate comments on ambiance, service, and food or present them in a particular order, but be specific in your details and examples. Use quotation marks for any descriptive phrases you borrow from the menu.

An example of a professional restaurant review, "Food, Service Hit and Miss at Gianno's," begins on page 110.

Short Story Review

Definition

A **short story** is a brief, imaginative narrative, with numerous functional elements (all of which can be analyzed): setting, conflict, characters, plot, theme, and point of view.

The overarching element of the short story is usually the plot. In the simplest terms, the plot begins when a character in a setting experiences (with or without being aware) a conflict. The plot develops as the character deals with the conflict in a single scene or sequence of scenes. All of this narrative is related from a first person (*I*) or a third person (*he, she, they*) point of view. The entire presentation has a theme, the underlying generalization or fictional point.

Short stories are fiction, meaning they are not a report of what has actually happened, though they may be based squarely on an author's experience.

Writing the Short Story Review

One theory about why we enjoy fiction—in print and film—is that we can analyze it. The events of our lives may often appear too complicated and close for us to figure out, but with fiction we can see connections more clearly. We can dissect fiction, examine the parts and their relationships, and speculate about what it all means. We can even relate fiction to our own experiences.

Like most writing, the short story review (analysis) is a combination of writing forms, but one form—analysis by division, comparison and contrast, cause and effect, or narration—may provide much of the pattern. For a short review, you will likely emphasize one aspect of the short story—setting, conflict, plot, character(s), theme, point of view—though you may touch on several.

- Develop your ideas by referring directly to the story; by explaining; and by using summaries, paraphrases, and quotations. Avoid the temptation to oversummarize.
- Use present tense in relating events in the story. For example, "Jude is trying to survive," not "Jude was trying to survive." Use quotation marks around the words you borrow and provide documentation if directed to do so by your instructor.
- Although a short story review is mainly analytical, it may include your speculation and call forth references to your personal experience.

Two short stories are included on the Student Website: "The Tell-Tale Heart" and "The Cask of Amontillado."

✳ Practicing Patterns of Analysis by Division

Exercise 1 Completing Patterns

Fill in the blanks in the following outlines to complete each analysis by division.

1. Unit: Doctor

    I. Principle: Effective as a general practitioner

    II. Parts based on the principle:

        A. Ability to _____

        B. Knowledge of _____

        C. Knowledge of computers and other equipment

2. Unit: Newspaper

    I. Principle: Sections for readers

    II. Parts based on the principle:

        A. News

        B. _____

        C. _____

        D. _____

        E. _____

✳ Examining Essays of Analysis by Division

Student Writer

Prison as a Community

Tanya

Tanya (not her real name) wrote this essay in a college English class at the California Institution for Women. By now some particulars may have changed. Double underlining is used to indicate transitional devices and parts of the unit being analyzed.

1   Few free-world citizens regard the California Institution for Women (CIW) as a walled city, but that is what it is. Before I was sent here, I imagined prison as a bunch of scared and scary people in a

Thesis
Subject of
analysis by
division

fenced pen. <u>Then I became a resident and discovered that, except for freedom, this place has all the parts of a community outside the fence</u>.

I. Government
(as laws)

It all begins with rules. CIW has a <u>government</u>, one that is totalitarian, not democratic. The constitution is a set of laws passed by the state of California. The warden and her associates administer the laws. The correctional officers enforce the laws. The convicts obey or else.

Topic
sentence and
transition

2   <u>These laws</u> also govern <u>where we live in the prison</u>. It is said that the two most important things in prison are <u>where</u>

II. Housing

<u>one lives</u> and where one works. An inmate's address at prison can be determined by several factors: behavior, reputation, age, and health. Therefore, one can be assigned to a cell block with designations such as ordinary (general dorm, room, or cell), honors, geriatrics, solitary, convalescent, protective custody, or

Example

psychiatric. At times special living units are formed. Once there was a living unit at CIW called the AIDs ward, for convicts who were HIV positive. If somebody approached these women as they were being escorted across the yard, a correctional

officer would blow a whistle and shout,
"Stay away! These inmates have AIDS! These
inmates have AIDS!" The HIV positive women
now live in housing for the general
population, and staff is more enlightened.

Topic sentence and transition 3   The <u>other part</u> of the saying "where
you work" is tied in with <u>both free-world
industry and the operation of the prison</u>.

III. Commerce and service
A. Offered work
For years CIW has produced clothing for
the California Transportation Agency
(CalTrans), made mostly of heavy orange
fabric. We have also manufactured Levis
and underwear for California prisons for
men. Most jobs relate to services, such as
food, laundry, maintenance, and clerical.
All able-bodied women, even those in
educational programs, must work. Some jobs
provide compensation, the so-called "pay
slots," but prison work is almost never
connected with vocational training or with
post-parole jobs. The money, usually about
fifteen to thirty dollars a month, is
placed in a trust fund and can be used in
the prison store for treats, smokes,
health aids, hygiene items, or the like.

Topic sentence and transition
B. Underground work
4   <u>Another part</u> of "work" at the prison
<u>relates to the underground activities and
economy</u>. The hustles include tattooing,

Examples   gambling, drugs, food running, laundry
service, strong-arming, body guarding, and
hootch (a homemade alcohol product)
making. That list tells you more about
prison than does the official line offered
to the public.

5   In addition to the commonplace housing
and the above and below ground work, CIW
IV. Religion   offers <u>religion</u> a la carte. Convicts have
A. Authorized   three full-time chaplains. Anyone can
attend a Jewish Seder, a Catholic Mass, or
a Protestant spectacular. Last Sunday, I
Example   attended a foot-stomping, woman-wailing
Gospel Bonanza put on by outside
evangelists, the men in spandex and the
women with big hair. The program rivaled
any free-world revival in a three-post
tent. Also available are sweat lodge
rituals for the Native Americans and
services for Muslims.

Topic   6   <u>Like the commercial</u> and service areas,
sentence and
transition   <u>religion has its underground activities.</u>
B. Unauthor-   Currently, an inmate, who was an ordained
ized
Example   minister on the streets, has been baptizing
women in the shower (total immersion, she
argues), marrying lesbians, and performing
exorcisms (including one on a schizoid
yard cat named Blue Eyes). Equally well

Example

known, a voodooist has recently constructed personalized images for putting a hex on those she believes have offended her, leading a number of terrified women to dispose of hair and other byproducts of personal hygiene only by the toilet flushing technique.

Topic 7
sentence and
transition
V. Education

A. Formal

Example

Another component of the community is school. It may be on an academically low level, such as literacy, or somewhat advanced, such as the GED program. At the practical level, in recent years, several vocational programs have been offered and then discontinued; plumbing, graphic arts, and hair styling. Small college programs, such as the one I am now enrolled in, depend on state funding, which in our case will be withdrawn next year.

Topic 8
sentence and
transition

B. Informal

Naturally, the other side of formal education at CIW is informal education. No one leaves the same as she was upon entering. Each inmate will learn from the prison and become either better or worse. I wish I could say that life improvement usually wins out over other forces. It does sometimes happen in this best of all criminal schools. For myself, against odds, I intend to make it so.

Conclusion 9	Yes, CIW is more than a holding pen
referring back	
to introduc-	for criminal types. <u>It really is a</u>
tion	

<u>community</u>. But being a social unit does

not make it a nice place to live. The

average person stays here for three to

five years and moves on, about the average

for movement on the street. And not all is

bad. Some of us convicts do save ourselves.

We occasionally get some help. For most,

the help is not enough.

Professional Writer

Food, Service Hit and Miss at Gianno's

John Batchelor, Special to the *Greensboro News & Record*

(Thursday, January 12, 2006 1:00 am)

John Batchelor is a freelance contributor to the Greensboro News & Record *who has been reviewing restaurants for more than 20 years. You can reach him at P.O. Box 20848, Greensboro NC 27420, or send e-mail to jebatchelor@netscape.net. To find his recent columns on the Internet, go to www.gotriad.com and click on dining. For older columns, click on News Archives.*

1   Renovations at Gianno's a couple of years ago have created a sort of Tuscan look, with wood beams overhead, beige stippled walls and tile floors. Seating is a bit crowded, and hard surfaces reflect sound, generating a noisy ambiance. This is a family-friendly restaurant, and the many children add to the volume.

2   A chalkboard at the entry describes the evening's specials but does not include prices. When we inquired, our server was not able to provide that information. Service in general proved problematic, ranging from slow but accurate to very slow with errors and omissions.

3   I could not help noticing a sign in the bar area: "This is not Burger King. You don't get it your way. You get it my way, or you don't get a damn thing." In an establishment that is supposed to

be in the hospitality business, this is a bad joke, and I don't think management should have allowed such a posting.

4   Gianno's began as a pizza specialty restaurant. My wife and I liked the firm, flavorful crust on Gianno's Pizza ($11.95). A mild tomato sauce hosted fresh mushrooms, onions, green peppers and black olives, plus sausage and pepperoni that tasted pretty much standard for area pizza.

5   Calamari ($6.95) provided a solid start to one evening's experience. The ample serving of thin-sliced rings and baby squid arrived crisp, hot and tender, with a tasty marinara sauce. The chopped spinach in Oysters Rockefeller ($6.95/six) didn't taste fresh. Most of the flavor came from the bacon and Parmesan cheese; there was no sauce, and the overall effect tilted toward the dry.

6   Entree prices include a house salad of iceberg lettuce, cucumber, red onion and Roma tomato slices—rather lean in comparison to other area restaurants, but at least a salad is included. Or you can upgrade ($1.95) to spinach salad with chopped tomato, red onion, a bacon product and toasted croutons.

7   Lasagna ($8.95) produced a good meaty flavor from ground beef, ricotta cheese and tomato sauce. This is an easy recommendation.

8   Veal Saltimbocca ($14.25) had been sauteed with bits of prosciutto, spinach and portabello mushrooms, then layered with melted mozzarella. The veal was a little firm, but acceptable at the price, and it tasted good. Spinach and ricotta cheese ravioli completed the presentation.

9   A chalkboard-posted Beef Tenderloin ($18.95) was ordered medium; it arrived well done, gray throughout, albeit still tender. No one checked back for satisfaction. We entered a complaint when the check arrived, and the manager came over and volunteered to delete the charge.

10   Two seafoods made positive impressions. Grilled Salmon ($15.95) was nice and moist, served in combination with eight medium-large deveined, tender shrimp over linguine. Capers, artichokes and diced tomatoes had been scattered on top, along with a dollop of lemon butter. Pecan Crusted Trout ($14.95) had been pan-fried, creating a delightfully crisp exterior; a light baking rendered the interior fully cooked yet moist. This was placed over rice with a dab of lemon butter.

11   We never received salads on one visit. The manager gave us a card for a free Italian Nachos appetizer on a return visit. Though

compensating somewhat for the omission, this procedure makes you come back in order to receive the free item as opposed to a procedure that makes you want to come back. Our waiter provided a free tiramisu—a custardy, chocolate-coffee flavored rendition that we really enjoyed.

12   On balance, some of the food at Gianno's would merit a return visit, some would not. I'm sure that if the service we received were typical, the restaurant would not have established the popular following that it has. But my experience cannot be ignored, hence a lower rating than I would have wished.

Gianno's Stone Oven
1124 Eastchester Drive
High Point
885-0762

Hours: 1 a.m.–11 p.m.
   Monday–Saturday
Sanitation grade: A (99.5)
Credit cards: Visa, MC, Discover
ABC permits: All
Appetizers: $4.95–$8.95
Soups: $2.25
Sandwiches: $5.95–$6.95
Handicapped accessibility:
   All seating on entry level
Kid friendly: Children's
   menu available
Healthy choices: Not identified
   on menu
Most recent visit: Dec. 22, 2005
Food:** Flavors abundant and
   enjoyable, usually

Pizza: $9.85–$12.95
Salads: $2.95–$7.98
Entrees: $7.75–$21.65, including
   salad
Desserts: Approximately $2.95–
   $3.95 (selections vary daily)
Theme: Casual Italian
Ambiance: Acceptable. Noisy,
   crowded.
Service: Acceptable. Slow,
   inattentive, error-filled.
Value: **½ Quantities are
   generous, prices very
   competitive
Overall rating: *

Exercise 2 Discussion and Critical Thinking

1. Which paragraph covers the ambiance (meaning the special atmosphere or mood created by the environment—the design, furnishings, sound, light, smell)?

2. Which paragraphs cover the quality and price of food?

3. Which paragraphs cover the quality of the service?

4. Does John Batchelor say how many times he visited Gianno's?

5. At a minimum, how many times should a reviewer visit a restaurant before evaluating it?

6. On what can readers base the credibility (accepting the person as an authority) of the reviewer; that is, why believe him or her?

7. Is one part of a review—ambiance, food, service—more important to you? If so, why?

✳ Topics for Essays of Analysis by Division

Reading-Related and Text-Based Topics

"Prison as a Community"

1. Write about another somewhat self-sufficient unit, such as a church, extended family, club, armed services, work unit, or gang. Explain how its parts make it a community.

"Food, Service Hit and Miss at Gianno's"

2. Write a paragraph or an essay in which you summarize and evaluate Batchelor's review. Would you have liked more elaboration on any of the main parts: ambiance, service, or food?

3. Using Batchelor's review as a model for discussing ambiance, service, and food, write a review of your own experience in a restaurant. Visit the restaurant one or two times. If you go with family members or friends, consider asking them to order different items from the menu. Then, before eating your food, increase the range of your sampling by tasting items (two small bites) from their plates (with their permission—perhaps rewarding them by offering to pay a small part of their check). Include specific information, using names and prices of food, examples of good or bad service, and descriptive details about the atmosphere.

4. If you have worked as a food server in a restaurant, analyze a party of more than eight you have served. Use three or more parts for your analysis by division. Consider behavior and politeness, cleanliness and neatness, and fairness and generosity in tipping.

Cross-Curricular Topics

5. For an essay topic pertaining to a current or former class other than English, select a unit that can be divided into parts. Consult your textbook(s) for ideas on that subject. Talk with your instructor(s) in other fields, especially those that relate to your major field of study. Your writing instructor may require you to photocopy a page or more of your source material if your work is largely summary. Following are a few examples from various disciplines:

- Art History: Points for analyzing a painting or other work of art
- Music History: Points for analyzing a musical composition or the performance of a musical composition
- Agriculture: Points for judging livestock
- History: Characteristics that made a historical figure great
- Government: Basic organization of the United Nations
- Biology: Working parts of an organ or organism
- Physical Education: Parts of a football team in a particular offensive or defensive formation
- Business: Structure of management for a particular business
- Law Enforcement: Organization of a specific precinct

Career-Related Topics

6. Explain how the parts of a particular product function as a unit.
7. Explain how each of several qualities of a specific person—intelligence, sincerity, knowledgeability, ability to communicate, manner, attitude, appearance—makes that individual an effective salesperson, manager, or employee.
8. Explain how the demands or requirements for a particular job represent a comprehensive picture of that job.
9. Explain how the aspects of a particular service (such as friendly, competent, punctual, confidential) work together in a satisfactory manner.

General Topics

Some of the following topics are too broad for an essay and should be narrowed. For example, the general "a wedding ceremony" could be narrowed to the particular "José and Maria's wedding ceremony." Divide your focused topic into parts and analyze it.

10. An organ in the human body
11. A machine such as an automobile, a computer, a camera
12. A ceremony—wedding, graduation
13. A holiday celebration, a pep rally, a sales convention, a religious revival
14. An offensive team in football (any team in any game)
15. A family, a relationship, a gang, a club, a sorority, a fraternity
16. A CD, a performance, a song, a singer, an actor, a musical group, a musical instrument
17. A movie, a television program, a video game
18. Any well-known person—athlete, politician, criminal, writer

✳ Writer's Guidelines at a Glance: Analysis by Division

Almost anything can be analyzed by division—for example, how the parts of the ear work in hearing, how the parts of the eye work in seeing, or how the parts of the heart work in pumping blood throughout the body. Subjects such as these are all approached with the same systematic procedure.

1. This is the procedure.

   - Step 1: Begin with something that is a unit.
   - Step 2: State the principle by which the unit can function.
   - Step 3: Divide the unit into parts according to that principle.
   - Step 4: Discuss each of the parts in relation to the unit.

2. This is the way you might apply that procedure to writing about a good boss.

▪ Step 1: Unit	Manager
▪ Step 2: Principle of function	Effective as a leader
▪ Step 3: Parts based on the principle	Fair, intelligent, stable, competent in the field
▪ Step 4: Discussion	Consider each part in relation to the person's effectiveness as a manager.

3. This is how a basic outline of analysis by division might look.

> *Thesis:* To be effective as a leader, a manager needs specific qualities.
>
> I. Fairness
> II. Intelligence
> III. Stability
> IV. Competence in the field

8

Process Analysis:
Writing About Doing

✳ Writing Essays of Process Analysis

If you have any doubt about how frequently we use process analysis, just think about how many times you have heard people say, "How do you do it?" or "How is [was] it done?" Even when you are not hearing those questions, you are posing them yourself when you need to make something, cook a meal, assemble an item, take some medicine, repair a toy, or figure out what happened. In your college classes, you may have to discover how osmosis occurs, how a rock changes form, how a mountain was formed, how a battle was won, or how a bill goes through the legislature.

If you need to explain how to do something or how something was (is) done, you will write a paper of **process analysis.** You will break down your topic into stages, explaining each so that your reader can duplicate or understand the process.

Two Types of Process Analysis:
Directive and Informative

The questions "How do I do it?" and "How is (was) it done?" will lead you into two different types of process analysis—directive and informative.

Directive process analysis explains how to do something. As the name suggests, it gives directions and tells the reader how to do something. It says, for example, "Read me, and you can bake a pie [tune up your car, solve a math problem, write an essay, take some medicine]." Because it is presented directly to the reader, it usually addresses the reader as "you," or it implies the "you" by saying something such as "First [you] purchase a large, fat wombat, and then [you] . . ." In the same way, this textbook addresses you or implies "you" because it is a long how-to-do-it (directive process analysis) statement.

Informative process analysis explains how something was (is) done by giving data (information). Whereas the directive process analysis tells you what to do in the future, the informative process analysis tells you what has occurred or what is occurring. If it is something in nature, such as the formation of a mountain, you can read and understand the process by which it emerged. In this type of process analysis, you do not tell the reader what to do; therefore, you do not use the words *you* or *your*.

Working with Stages
Preparation

In the first stage of writing directive process analysis, list the materials or equipment needed for the process and discuss the necessary setup arrangements. For some topics, this stage will also provide technical terms and definitions. The degree to which this stage is detailed will depend on both the subject itself and the expected knowledge and experience of the projected audience.

Informative process analysis may begin with background or context rather than with preparation. For example, a statement explaining how mountains form might begin with a description of a flat portion of the earth made up of plates that are arranged like a jigsaw puzzle.

Steps

The actual process will be presented here. Each step must be explained clearly and directly, and phrased to accommodate the audience. The language, especially in directive process analysis, is likely to be simple and concise; however, avoid dropping words such as *and, a, an, the,* and *of,* and thereby lapsing into "recipe language." In directive process analysis the steps may be accompanied by explanations about why certain procedures are necessary and how not following directions carefully can lead to trouble. In informative process analysis the steps should appear in a logical progression within a sequence.

Order

The order will usually be chronological (time based) in some sense. Certain transitional words are commonly used to promote coherence: *first, second, third, then, soon, now, next, finally, at last, therefore, consequently,* and—especially for informative process analysis—words used to show the passage of time such as hours, days of the week, and so on.

Basic Forms

Consider using this form for **directive process analysis** (with topics such as how to cook something or how to fix something).

  I. Preparation
    A.
    B.
    C.
 II. Steps
    A.
    B.
    C.
    D.

Consider using this form for **informative process analysis** (with topics such as how a volcano functions or how a battle was won).

  I. Background or context
    A.
    B.
    C.
 II. Change or development (narrative)
    A.
    B.
    C.
    D.

✳ Practicing Patterns of Process Analysis

Exercise 1 Completing Patterns

Using directive process analysis, fill in the blanks in the following outline for replacing a flat tire with the spare. Work in a group if possible.

  I. Preparation

    A. Park car.

    B. _____

   C. Obtain car jack.

   D. _____

   E. _____

II. Steps

   A. Remove hub cap (if applicable).

   B. Loosen lug nuts a bit.

   C. _____

   D. _____

   E. Remove wheel with flat tire.

   F. _____

   G. _____

   H. Release jack pressure.

   I. _____

✳ Examining Essays of Process Analysis

Student Writer

The Skinny on Working for a Dermatologist

J. Kim Birdine

After having traveled a long way from a Korean orphanage to the United States, J. Kim Birdine is still on the move. In writing this essay of process analysis, she demonstrates the same intellectual qualities she uses so well in her role as an assistant to a doctor, both in the office and in the operating room.

Author's role
Double underlining indicates the use of transitional devices.

1   As a medical assistant for a dermatologist, I am actively involved in every aspect of the practice, recommending products, doing laser treatments for veins, and administering skin peels. The

younger patients generally see the doctor
to correct their skin problems, whether
they're suffering from a persistent dry
patch, uneven skin tone, or a bout with
acne. A good number of the patients come
in for cosmetic reasons, wanting their
wrinkles smoothed out or their dark

Thesis   blotches lasered off. <u>The most important</u>
<u>part of my job, though, is to prepare</u>
<u>surgical trays for the patients with skin</u>
<u>cancer and to assist the doctor through</u>
<u>the procedure.</u>

I. Preparation   2   My <u>initial concern</u> when <u>setting up a</u>
<u>surgical tray</u> is that everything is

1   <u>sterile</u>. This means that all the <u>metal</u>
<u>instruments</u>, <u>gauze</u>, and <u>applicators</u>
(Q-Tips) are <u>put through</u> an <u>Autoclave</u>

2   (steam sterilizer), to ensure

**Order
by time**   sterilization. Once everything is sterile,
<u>I begin setting up</u> my <u>surgical tray by</u>
<u>placing a sterile field on a tray</u>, which
has long legs and wheels at the base so
that it can be rolled. The <u>tray</u> should
<u>stand</u> about <u>waist high</u> so the physician
can reach the instruments easily. The
sterile field is a large white tissue that
I carefully take out of a sealed pack,
touching it only at the corners to unfold

it to its full size. It serves as a base
on which to place all the instruments.

Transition   3   3   <u>Next</u> all of the <u>metal instruments</u> are
placed on the <u>tray</u> with a long-handled

Details: "pick-up." The <u>necessary instruments</u> are a
Specific words   <u>scalpel, a skin hook, large forceps, small</u>
<u>forceps, straight scissors, curved</u>
<u>scissors, a large needle holder</u>, and a
<u>small needle holder</u>. All are placed with
handles facing toward me, except the small
needle holder and the straight scissors.
These two should be positioned at a corner
away from me with the handles facing out.

Why   The <u>position</u> of all <u>of</u> the <u>instruments</u> is
procedure is   <u>important so that the doctor can reach</u>
important   <u>them with ease</u>. The ones placed in the
corner are for me to use while assisting
with suturing. A surgical tray is <u>not</u>
<u>complete without</u> a small <u>stack of gauze</u>
(large) and <u>about twenty applicators</u>. The
entire tray is covered with another
sterile field exactly like the one placed
initially on the tray.

Transition   4   4   <u>Just prior</u> to surgery, <u>I set up extras</u>.
I <u>place on</u> the <u>counter anesthesia</u>--a 3cc
syringe of lidocaine with epinephrine--<u>and</u>
a <u>disinfectant skin cleanser</u>, along with
<u>two pair of surgical gloves</u>, one for the

5   doctor and one for me. <u>I turn on</u> the
     <u>hyfrecator</u>, which is a cauterizer used to
     stop bleeding by burning the tissue. <u>I</u>

6   <u>prepare</u> a <u>specimen bottle</u> indicating on
     its label the patient's name, the date,
     the doctor's name, and the area of the
     body from which the specimen is taken. <u>I</u>

7   <u>remove</u> the <u>sterile field</u> <u>on top of</u> the
     <u>instruments</u> and <u>place</u> the <u>sutures</u>
     requested by the doctor and a <u>different</u>
     <u>kind of sterile field</u>, which has a hole in

Reason for   the middle of it, <u>on the tray</u>. <u>This field</u>
procedure   <u>enables the doctor to place the hole</u>
     <u>directly over the surgery site</u>, exposing
     the area to be worked on and covering the
     surrounding areas.

II. Transition   5   <u>During</u> surgery, once the doctor
steps   removes the section that needs to be

1   tested, <u>I place it in</u> the <u>specimen jar</u>,
     <u>seal the lid</u> on it, and <u>place it on</u> the
     <u>counter</u>. I have to be attentive to the
     surgery at this point to assist in

2   reducing the bleeding. <u>My job is to apply</u>
     <u>gauze or applicators wherever bleeding</u>
     <u>occurs</u> and to <u>ready the hyfrecator in case</u>
     the <u>doctor needs it</u>. When bleeding is
     minimized, the doctor begins suturing. At
     this point I have the small needle holder

in hand as well as the straight scissors.

3   I use the small needle holder to grab the tip of the needle after the doctor inserts it through the skin, to pull it through for her. This makes her job easier. I use the straight scissors to cut the suture once she is finished with knotting. Sometimes she does some internal suturing

4   for the tissue under the skin, with dissolvable thread, and knots each turn. This is when I cut directly on top of the knot. The surface suturing is usually knotted at the beginning and at the end of the line of sutures and needs cutting down to one-quarter of an inch.

Transition   5   6   After surgery, I use peroxide to clean the patient's surgical site. I apply either a pressure bandage or a plain Band-Aid with antibiotic ointment. The pressure bandage is applied usually when there is a concern of more bleeding post surgery. I

6   explain to the patient how to take care of the surgical area and when to come back to have the sutures removed. This makes my

Concludes essay and re-flects back on introduction   job complete, until it is time for another set-up, when I will repeat the same process of ensuring a sterile environment for the patient.

Professional Writer

Fast, Sleek, and Shiny: Using the Internet to Help Buy New Cars

Preston Gralla

> *In his essay adapted from* The Complete Idiot's Guide to Online Shopping, *Preston Gralla presents down-to-earth advice on how to shop for a car on the Internet and how to avoid getting taken. Cars are only one of the many products featured in this book. This essay includes a discussion on how to buy a car and finance it, all through using your computer.*

1   Whether or not you plan to buy your new car over the Internet, make sure to do your prepurchase research online. Use the Internet to help decide which car to buy and to get the best deal possible from the dealer—or even to buy online. You'll get pleasure not only out of saving money, but also out of seeing car dealers gnash their teeth over the thought of how you were able to bargain them down to very little profit. There goes their trip to Cancun this year!

Step 1: Go Online to Research and Find Your Dream Machine

2   Your clunker has finally spit the last bit of black exhaust out of its tail pipe, and it's time to get a new dream machine. But what should you get? Should it be a supermacho, ego-enhancing sports utility vehicle? A trusty family station wagon? A hell-bent-for-leather sports car? Or just a plain old sedan? And which is the best model for your needs and pocketbook?

3   You'll find many sites to help you narrow down what you should buy. If you're not quite sure what you want, immediately head to the GTE Superpages Consumer Guide at www.consumer guide.com. Use the Interactive Car Finder—think of it as the "Complete Idiot's Guide to Choosing a Car." You select the kind of car (compact, sports utility vehicle, and so on), the price range, fuel economy, and features such as air-conditioning, and voilà—you'll get a list of cars that match your pocketbook and the features you want.

4   Car aficionados who want to know what the insiders think about cars should head to the online site of *Car and Driver* magazine at www.caranddriver.com. As you might guess, many, many more car sites online can help you decide which car to buy,

and many also offer car reviews. I'd suggest that after you use the Consumer Guide and the *Car and Driver* site to narrow down your choices, you check in with as many sites as possible to get their takes on the cars of your dreams. One excellent site is Edmunds at www.edmunds.com.

Step 2: Get Ready to Bargain—Find Out the True Dealer Invoice Price

5   Sure, the last time you bought a car, you probably thought you got a pretty good deal. The dealer may even have said something like, "You got the best of me that time, Buddy." Guess what? The dealer was lying. (What a shock!) You got taken for a ride. The dealer got the best of you. And it's not because you're not smart enough to drive a good bargain. It's because the dealer knows exactly how much the car cost, and you don't have a clue. Sticker price, retail price, rebates, MSRP (what in the world does that stand for, anyway?—oh, yeah, Manufacturer's Suggested Retail Price), the costs of all the "extras" (such as doors and an engine, it seems)—trying to put it all together makes your head start to spin. The whole pricing scheme for new cars is designed to confuse you. So what's a poor car buyer to do?

6   It's simple. Head to the Internet and find out exactly how much the dealer paid for the car (the dealer cost) to the dollar—including all the extras. When you're armed with that information, you can force the dealer to meet your price—or you can walk out the door and find a dealer who *will* meet it.

7   You can find the dealer invoice price at a number of sites on the Internet. But head to www.edmunds.com to get the best lowdown. It not only provides the most comprehensive information but also explains the ins and outs of car pricing, which is arcane enough to have confused a medieval philosopher. This site offers excellent how-to-buy articles as well.

8   The MSRP is the car's base price that the dealer will quote to you. Never, ever, ever pay that price for a car. If you do, the dealer and salesperson will be breaking out the champagne after you leave.

9   Find the invoice price. That's the most important number on the page. It's the price that the dealer pays the manufacturer for the base model of the car, without any extras. That's the num-

ber you're going to use when you start to bargain. Do you notice something interesting about the MSRP price and the invoice price? I thought you did; you have sharp eyes. The MSRP (sticker) price is several thousand dollars higher than the invoice price. So if a dealer knocks off $1,000 from the sticker price, you might think you're getting a good deal, but you're not—the dealer is still making out like a bandit.

10   Next, check out the invoice prices of the options you want— things like automatic transmission, a luggage rack, and a stereo. As you can see, each item has an MSRP as well as an invoice price, which means that the dealer is making money by marking up all your extras as well. The dealer also has to pay a destination charge, which can be $500 or more. Edmunds reports that charge as well.

11   To figure out the true cost to the dealer of the car you're interested in buying, do this math:

$$\text{Invoice Price + Invoice Price of Extras +}$$
$$\text{Destination Charge = Dealer's Costs}$$

Now here's a strange fact: Even if you pay only the dealer's invoice costs for a car, in most instances the dealer *still* makes a profit. That's because of a little-known program called the "Dealer Hold Back." The dealer hold back is a percentage of the MSRP of the vehicle, including all extras. When a dealer sells a vehicle, the manufacturer sends the dealer a check based on the hold back percentage and the MSRP of the vehicle. Domestic carmakers typically pay a 3 percent dealer hold back, and foreign makers often pay 2 percent. But the amount varies from manufacturer to manufacturer. Edmunds tells you the dealer hold back for the car you're buying.

12   Let's take an example. Say the MSRP of the car and extras you've bought is $25,000, and the dealer hold back is 3 percent. According to this formula, after you buy the car, the manufacturer sends the dealer a check for $750. Therefore, even if the dealer sells the car at invoice price, he or she is still making money. Note, though, that the money doesn't go to your salesperson—it goes straight to the dealer. So, no salesperson is going to agree to give you a car at invoice price.

13   Another way to save hundreds or even thousands of dollars when buying your next car is to find out what kinds of rebates

and dealer incentives are available; on the www.edmunds.com site, just click on Incentives and Rebates.

Step 3: Psyching Out Your Dealer with Information You Got Online

14   So now you know the invoice cost of the car you want to buy, the destination charge, the dealer hold back, and any kinds of rebates and incentives available on the car you're interested in buying. What next? Let's say you want to buy a car from a dealer, not through the Web.

15   First, print everything out directly from the Web so that you have a sheaf of papers you can refer to. When you walk in with the printouts, the dealer will realize you know your business and won't try to pull a fast one on you. (Well, the dealer may *try* to pull a fast one, but won't be able to succeed.)

16   Also, figure out on a sheet of paper how much you're willing to pay for the car. Base it on the invoice price of the car. You should hold the line at 3 percent over invoice cost if you can—and if the car isn't very popular or new models are about to come out, try to get it at 2 percent or less over invoice cost. If you're looking to buy a hot-selling car, you might not be able to drive such a hard bargain, but it's worth a try. For cars that aren't moving fast, you should be able to bargain down to your 2 percent or 3 percent figure. Also, when figuring the price you should pay for a car, be sure to consider any rebates or incentives.

Exercise 2 Discussion and Critical Thinking

1. Is this essay informative or directive?

2. Sometimes the preparation stage is implied or assumed. To shop on the Internet, of course, a person needs a computer with Internet access. Does Gralla specify the preparation stage, or does he simply make an assumption about the computer and Internet access?

3. Gralla gives much information, but he also is writing with a particular audience in mind. Just what does he expect the reader to know about computers?

4. How many steps does Gralla use?

5. In tone (the way the author regards the subject and the reader), what distinguishes this essay from many directive process analysis statements?

✳ Topics for Essays of Process Analysis

Reading-Related and Text-Based Topics

"The Skinny on Working for a Dermatologist"

1. Using this essay as a model, write about a job that required you to play an important supporting role. Explain both how you helped and what the other person did.
2. Write about a job that required you to play a leading role.

"Fast, Sleek, and Shiny: Using the Internet to Help Buy New Cars"

3. Use the form on pages 47–50 to outline this essay.
4. Write a summary of or a two-part response to this essay. (See Chapter 1 for an example.)
5. Use the information in this essay to write a reaction in which you evaluate the last time you or someone you know purchased a car. Go point by point from the decision to buy a particular car to the actual purchase. Refer to and quote from the essay as you explain what went right and what could have gone better if the buyer had done some Internet homework.
6. Following the directions in this essay, conduct an actual search for a desirable car. Explain what happened as you performed the process explained by Gralla. Refer directly to and quote from the essay.

Cross-Curricular Topics

7. Write an essay about a procedure you follow in your college work in a science (chemistry, biology, geology) lab. You may explain

how to analyze a rock, how to dissect something, how to operate something, or how to perform an experiment.
8. Write an essay about how to do something in an activity or performance class, such as drama, physical education, art, or music.

Career-Related Topics

9. Explain how to display, package, sell, or demonstrate a product.
10. Explain how to perform a service or to repair or install a product.
11. Explain the procedure for operating a machine, computer, piece of equipment, or other device.
12. Explain how to manufacture or construct something.
13. Explain how to update or modernize a style, product, or concept.

General Topics

Most of the following topics are directive as they are phrased. However, each can be transformed into a how-it-was-done informative topic by personalizing it and explaining stage by stage how you, someone else, or a group did something. For example, you could write either a directive process analysis about how to deal with an obnoxious person or an informative process analysis about how you or someone else dealt with an obnoxious person. The two types of process analysis are often blended, especially in the personal approach. Many of the following topics will be more interesting to you and your readers if they are personalized.

Select one of the following topics and write a process-analysis essay about it. Most of the topics require some narrowing to be treated in an essay. For example, writing about playing baseball is too broad; writing about how to bunt may be manageable.

14. How to end a relationship without hurting someone's feelings
15. How to pass a test for a driver's license
16. How to get a job at _____
17. How to eat _____
18. How to perform a magic trick
19. How to repair _____
20. How to assemble _____
21. How to learn about another culture
22. How to approach someone you would like to know better
23. How to make a videotape of a particular event

✳ Writer's Guidelines at a Glance: Process Analysis

1. Decide whether your process analysis is mainly directive or informative, and be consistent in using pronouns and other designations.

   - Use second person for the directive analysis as you address the reader (use *you, your*).
   - Use first person for the informative analysis; do not address the reader (use *I*).
   - Use third person for the informative analysis; do not address the reader (use *he, she, it, they, them, individuals,* the name of your subject).

2. Consider using this form for the directive process analysis (with topics such as how to cook something or how to fix something).

   I. Preparation
      A.
      B.
      C.
   II. Steps
      A.
      B.
      C.
      D.

3. Consider using this form for the informative process analysis (with topics such as how a volcano functions or how a battle was won).

   I. Background or context
      A.
      B.
      C.
   II. Change or development (narrative)
      A.
      B.
      C.
      D.

4. In explaining the stages and using technical terms, take into account whether your audience will be mainly well informed, moderately informed, or poorly informed.

5. Use transitional words indicating time or other progression (such as *finally, at last, therefore, consequently,* and—especially for the informative process analysis—words showing passage of time, such as hours, days of the week, and so on).
6. Avoid recipe language; do not drop *the, a, an,* or *of.*

9

Cause and Effect:
Determining
Reasons
and Results

✳ Writing Essays of Cause and Effect

Causes and effects deal with reasons and results; they are sometimes discussed together and sometimes separately. Like other forms of writing to explain, writing about causes and effects is based on natural thought processes. The shortest, and arguably the most provocative, poem in the English language—"I/Why?"—is posed by an anonymous author about cause. Children are preoccupied with delightful and often exasperating "why" questions. Daily we encounter all kinds of causes and effects. The same subject may raise questions of both kinds.

> The car won't start. *Why?* (cause)
> The car won't start. *What now?* (effect)

At school, from the biology lab to the political-science classroom, and at work, from maintaining relationships to changing procedures, causes and effects are found everywhere.

Organizing Cause and Effect

One useful approach to developing a cause-and-effect analysis is **listing.** Write down the event, situation, or trend you are concerned about. Then, on the left side of the page list the causes and on the right side list the effects. Here is an example.

133

Causes	Event, Situation, or Trend	Effects
Low self-esteem		Life of crime
Drugs		Drug addiction
Tradition	*Joining*	Surrogate family relationship
Fear	*a gang*	Protection
Lacking family		Ostracism
Needs protection		Restricted vocational opportunities
Neighborhood status		

As you use prewriting techniques to explore your ideas, you need to decide whether your topic should mainly inform or mainly persuade. If you intend to inform, your tone should be coolly objective. If you intend to persuade, your tone should be subjective. In either case, you should take into account the views of your audience as you phrase your ideas. You should also take into account how much your audience understands about your topic and develop your ideas accordingly.

Composing the Thesis

Now that you have organized your ideas under causes and effects, you are ready to focus on the causes, on the effects, or, occasionally, on both.

Your controlling idea, or thesis, might be one of causes: "People join gangs for three main reasons." Later, as you use the idea as a thesis in an essay, you would rephrase it to make it less mechanical, allowing it to become part of the flow of your discussion. If you wanted to personalize the work—thereby probably making it more interesting—you could write about someone you know who joined a gang. And you could use the same basic framework, the three causes, to indicate why this particular person joined a gang.

Your selection of a thesis takes you to the next writing phase: that of completing an outline or outline alternative. There you need to consider three closely related points:

- Review the kinds of causes and effects.
- Evaluate the importance of sequence.
- Introduce ideas and work with patterns.

Considering Kinds of Causes and Effects

Causes and effects can be primary or secondary, immediate or remote.

Primary or Secondary

Primary means "major," and **secondary** means "minor." A primary cause may be sufficient to bring about the situation (subject). For example, infidelity may be a primary (and possibly sufficient by itself) cause of divorce for some people but not for others, who regard it as secondary. Or if country X is attacked by country Y, the attack itself, as a primary cause, may be sufficient to bring on a declaration of war. A diplomatic blunder regarding visas for workers may be of secondary importance and, although significant, would not be reason enough to start a war.

Immediate or Remote

Causes and effects often occur at a distance in time or place from the situation. The immediate effect of sulfur in the atmosphere may be atmospheric pollution, but the long-range, or remote, effect may be acid rain and the loss of species. The immediate cause of the greenhouse effect may be the depletion of the ozone layer, whereas the long-range, or remote, cause is the use of CFCs (commonly called *Freon,* which are found in such items as Styrofoam cups). Even more remote, the ultimate cause may be the people who use the products containing Freon. Your purpose will determine the causes and effects appropriate for your essay.

Evaluating the Importance of Sequence

The sequence in which events occur(red) may or may not be significant. When you are dealing with several sequential events, determine whether the sequence of events has causal connections; that is, does one event bring about another?

Consider this sequence of events: Joe's parents get divorced, and Joe joins a gang. We know that one reason for joining a gang is to gain family companionship. Therefore, we may conclude that Joe joined the gang to satisfy his need for family companionship, which he lost when his parents divorced. But if we do so, we may have reached a wrong conclusion, because Joe's joining the gang after the family breakup does not necessarily mean that the two events are related. Maybe Joe joined the gang because of drug dependency, low self-esteem, or a need for protection.

In each case, examine the connections. To assume that one event is *caused* by another just because it *follows* the other is a logical error called a *post hoc* ("after this") fallacy. An economic depression may occur after a president takes office, but that does not necessarily mean the depression was caused by the new administration. It might have occurred anyway, perhaps in an even more severe form.

Order

The order of the causes and effects you discuss in your paper may be based on time, space, emphasis, or a combination:

- **Time:** If one stage leads to another, as in a discussion of the causes and effects of upper atmospheric pollution, your paper would be organized best by time.
- **Space:** In some instances causes and effects are organized best by their relation in space. For instance, the causes of an economic recession could be discussed in terms of local factors, regional factors, national factors, and international factors.
- **Emphasis:** Some causes and effects may be more important than others. For instance, if some causes of divorce are primary (perhaps infidelity and physical abuse) and others are secondary (such as annoying habits and laziness), a paper about divorce could present the secondary causes first, and then move on to primary causes to emphasize the latter as more important.

In some instances, two or more factors (such as time and emphasis) may be linked; in that case, select the order that best fits what you are trying to say, or combine orders.

Introducing Ideas and Working with Patterns

In introducing your controlling idea—probably in an introductory paragraph—you will almost certainly want to perform two functions:

1. *Discuss your subject.* For example, if you are writing about the causes or effects of divorce, begin with a statement about divorce as a subject.
2. *Indicate whether you will concentrate on causes or effects or a combination.* That indication should be made clear early in the essay. Concentrating on one—causes or effects—does not mean you will not mention the other; it only means you will emphasize one of them. You can lend emphasis to your main concern(s), causes, effects, or a combination, by repeating key words such as *cause, reason, effect, result, consequence,* and *outcome.*

The most likely pattern for your work is shown in Figure 9.1.

Figure 9.1
Patterns of Cause and Effect

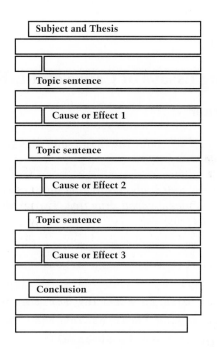

✳ **Practicing Patterns of Cause and Effect**

Exercise 1 Completing Patterns

Fill in the blanks to complete first the causes outline and then the effects outline.

    1. Causes for dropping out of high school

       I. Family tradition

      II. _____

     III. _____

     IV. _____

2. Effects of getting a college education

   I. Better informed

   II. _____

   III. _____

   IV. _____

✳ Examining Essays of Cause and Effect

Student Writer

Getting High and Living Low

Sergio Ramos

Sergio Ramos writes about growing up in a school rife with ille-gal drugs. Ramos escaped drug free. Two of his friends were less fortunate.

1   The use of drugs and alcohol from grade school through high school has been a major concern in recent years. Myriads of young kids turn to stealing for the means of satisfying their addictions. The high school dropout rate is at an all-time high across the nation, and one of the main causes is alcohol and drug abuse. Most of the convicts in prison were locked up because of drug-related crimes. <u>The repeated use of drugs and alcohol at an early age sets a pattern and leads to failure during adulthood; that's what happened to some of my close friends.</u>

Thesis

2   I had a friend named Gerardo who drank beer and smoked marijuana when he was in the fifth grade. He was influenced by his older brother Luis. The only thing that Gerardo talked about at school all day was that he could not wait to get home to smoke marijuana

Effect

with his brother in their clubhouse. I lived next door, and I would usually go over to watch them get high. They constantly attempted to convince me to try it, but to their dismay, they always failed. Once it was time for Gerardo to do his homework, he would eagerly ask me for help. When Gerardo was sent to the store to buy items for his mother, he would usually steal the items and keep the money to buy beer or marijuana.

3

Effect

When I got to junior high school, I really began to notice the heavy use of drugs and alcohol. I saw students "snort" cocaine behind their open books in class while the teachers wrote notes on the board. I also saw students smoking angel dust on the physical education field during lunchtime. They brought alcoholic beverages on campus and many students smoked a joint before their classes began. Most of these youngsters eventually were caught and expelled from school. Luis was a football player in high school while Gerardo and I were in junior high. Luis "snorted" half a gram of cocaine before every game he played. Gerardo had begun to sniff typewriter correction fluid just for fun.

4

Effect

Once when we were in the eighth grade, we decided we were going to smoke a marijuana cigarette with two girls from school. After school, at the clubhouse, we could not find the joint we had promised the girls. I felt extremely happy that I was not going to go through with it. Then the two girls began to get upset, and said we had lied to them. Gerardo immediately handed each of them a sandwich bag with typewriter correction fluid

Cause

inside. After the three of them began inhaling the substance, they began behaving erratically. Then one of the girls, whom I had an extremely strong crush on, handed me her bag and asked me to try it. I had never felt peer pressure as strong as I did that day. I hesitated at first, but after she

Effect

moved close and kissed me, I felt obligated to try. It was the worst hallucinating effect I have ever experienced. Gerardo began crawling on the ground because he could not walk, and we all laughed at him.

5   Luis and Gerardo both dropped out of high school because of their addiction to drugs.

Effects

They both became crack addicts, and Luis was also an alcoholic. Gerardo ended up in prison for robbery, which he did often in order to support his expensive drug habit. After his release, he went through counseling and treatment, and he was able to stop smoking crack, but he still drinks beer and smokes marijuana. Luis remains a crack addict and an alcoholic. He continues to live at home, and he refuses to get treatment for his disease. Working as a security guard, he spends his entire paycheck on drugs and alcohol. These are only two examples of the tragedies that exist all across this nation.

Professional Writer

The Ghetto Made Me Do It

Francis Flaherty

This essay by freelance author Francis Flaherty was first published in In These Times, *a biweekly magazine from Chicago.*

1   When Felicia "Lisa" Morgan was growing up, her parents would sit down to meals with guns next to their plates. They were defending themselves—against each other.

2   "This was Lisa's dinner," explains attorney Robin Shellow. "She was seven at the time."

3   If nothing else, Lisa Morgan's childhood in a poor, inner-city Milwaukee neighborhood starkly illustrates the tragic effects of omnipresent urban violence. "Mom shot dad," Shellow says. "And Mom shot boyfriend. . . . [Lisa's] uncle, who was actually her age, was murdered. Two days later, her other uncle was murdered. Her sister's boyfriend was paralyzed from the neck down by gunfire. Her brother was shot at and injured. Her mother once had set her father on fire."

4   If this weren't enough tragedy in one young life, Lisa Morgan's mother was a drug addict and Lisa was raped at age 12.

The "Ghetto Defense"

5   So perhaps it's not too surprising that Morgan, as a teenager, committed six armed robberies and one intentional homicide in the space of 17 minutes in October 1991. The victims were girls; the stolen objects were jewelry, shoes and a coat. The dead girl was shot at point-blank range.

6   What *is* surprising—to the legal establishment, at least—is the approach Robin Shellow used in defending Morgan. In the girl's neighborhood and in her family, Shellow argued, violence is a *norm*, an occurrence so routine that Morgan's 17 years of exposure to it have rendered her not responsible for her actions.

7   This "ghetto defense" proved fruitless in Morgan's case. In court, the young woman was found both sane and guilty. Unless Shellow wins on appeal, Morgan will be behind bars well into [this] century.

8   But despite its failure for Morgan, Shellow's "cultural psychosis" or "psychosocial history" strategy has taken hold. "I've gotten hundreds of calls from interested attorneys," Shellow says. Already, the defense is being floated in courtrooms around the nation. It's eliciting both enthusiasm and outrage.

The Defense Is a Medical One

9   Technically, Shellow's defense is a medical one. She believes that Morgan suffers from post traumatic stress disorder (PTSD)

and other psychological ailments stemming from her lifelong exposure to violence.

10   Like other good lawyers, Shellow knows that the law abhors broadly applicable excuses, so she emphasizes the narrowness of her claim. Morgan belongs to a very small group of inner-city residents with "tremendous intra-familial violence," only some of whom might experience PTSD. She also stresses the unrevolutionary nature of the defense, medically and legally. PTSD has been recognized as a malady in standard diagnostic texts since 1980, she says, and it has been employed as a criminal defense for Vietnam veterans, battered wives and many other trauma victims.

11   Despite Shellow's attempts to show that her defense is neither new nor broad, the case is ringing loud alarms. For, however viewed, her strategy sets up an inflammatory equation between inner-city conditions and criminal exculpation. The implication is that if you grew up in a poor, violent neighborhood and you commit a crime, you may go scot-free.

12   Yet why not a ghetto defense? After all, if a Vietnam veteran can claim PTSD from the shock of war, why shouldn't a similar defense be available for a young black reared in the embattled precincts of Bed-Stuy [Bedford-Stuyvesant neighborhood of New York City]? Sounds sensible, no? Isn't a ghetto like a battlefield?

Compare These Neighborhoods to War Zones

13   Alex Kotlowitz, who chronicled the lives of two Chicago black boys in *There Are No Children Here*, goes even further. He says the inner city can be worse than war. "You hear constant comparisons of these neighborhoods to war zones, but I think there are some pretty significant differences," he says. "In war, there's at least a sense that someday there will be a resolution, some vision that things could be different. That is not the case in the inner cities. There is no vision. And there's no sense of who's friend and who's foe."

14   There are other analogies that make the ghetto defense seem very legitimate. For instance, despite traditional self-defense principles, a battered wife in some jurisdictions can kill her sleeping husband and be legally excused for the homicide. The reason is the psychological harm she has sustained from her life of fear and violence.

15   Why not Lisa Morgan? Hasn't her life been debilitatingly violent and fearful?

16   These arguments make some lawyers hopeful about the future of Shellow's pioneering strategy. But most observers are pessimistic. "We'll get nowhere with it," says famous defense lawyer William Kunstler.

The Poor Instead of the Powerful

17   Why? One reason is that the American justice system often favors the powerful over the poor. For generations, for instance, the bloodiest crime in the nation—drunk driving—was punished with a relative wrist slap. By contrast, a recent federal law mandates that those convicted of the new crime of carjacking get socked with a minimum and mandatory 15-year sentence.

18   What explains these disparate approaches? Simple: protection of the affluent classes. Light penalties for drunk driving protect the affluent because they often drive drunk. Harsh carjacking penalties protect the affluent because they are the usual carjacking victims. "The middle class sees carjacking [laws] as protecting them from people coming out of some poor neighborhood and just showing up in *their* neighborhood and committing a crime in which they are at risk of dying," says Professor James Liebman of Columbia University School of Law.

19   Because the ghetto defense protects the poor instead of the powerful, Kunstler and others doubt it has a bright future. Other factors further dim the strategy's chances. Fear is a main one, says Professor Liebman. The ghetto defense brings a gulp from jurors because "their first thought is, 'If he's not responsible, then none of those people are,'" he reasons. And we all know what that means: riots, mayhem, Los Angeles.

20   Social guilt raises even higher the hurdles for the ghetto defense. To allow such a defense is a tacit admission that we—society—tolerate a situation so hobbling that its victims have become unaccountable for their actions. "If it ain't them who's guilty, it's us," says Michael Dowd, director of the Pace University Battered Women's Justice Center in New York. And "it's just too horrific for us to accept responsibility, too horrific to say, 'I'm responsible for what happened in L.A.' We will be able to accept the [ghetto] defense at the same moment that we are seriously moved to eradicate the realities behind that defense."

21   What are the biggest criticisms of the ghetto defense? One focuses on the victim's identity. Battered spouses and battered children are accused of killing precisely those who hurt them. This endows the crime with a certain rough justice. But in a ghetto defense case, the victim is usually an innocent stranger.

22   Others, like Kotlowitz, worry that the ghetto defense might dislodge the cornerstone of our justice system: personal responsibility. "We have to be careful not to view people growing up in neighborhoods completely as victims; they are both victims and actors," he warns. "We can't absolve them from responsibility."

23   Lisa Morgan "went up to someone she didn't know, stole a jacket from her, and then just blew her away," he says. "There's no way as a society that we can excuse that. We can understand it, but we can't excuse it."

24   He raises a fundamental question. Everyone can point to scars from the past—alcoholic parents, tragic love, etc.—and claim exculpation. And if all are excused, who is responsible?

25   Another worry is diminished standards. "[The ghetto defense] lowers expectations," Kotlowitz continues, "It says, 'OK, I understand what you've been through, so it's OK to go out and hurt somebody.' And once you lower your expectations, particularly with kids, they will meet only those lower expectations."

A Disease Is a Disease

26   It's only fair to note that other criminal defenses also have these weaknesses. For instance, the victim of a PTSD-afflicted veteran is often an innocent passerby, and the battered-spouse doctrine certainly raises questions about personal responsibility and lowered expectations.

27   And if, as seems likely, some ghetto residents do have PTSD largely as a result of their living conditions, it's hard to see why this ailment should be exculpatory for veterans, say, but not for ghetto residents. After all, a disease is a disease, and how you got it is irrelevant.

28   How deep go the wounds from the ghetto? Here are two incidents in Morgan's life: "When Felicia was about 11, her mother put a knife to her throat and threatened to kill her," according to a psychologist's report in the case. "Felicia escaped by running into the basement, where she 'busted the lights out with my hand' so that her mother could not see her." Then, when she was 12, the landlord attacked her. "Felicia fought him off by throwing

hot grease onto him, but he finally subdued her, tied her hands to the bed, stuffed her mouth with a sock and raped her."

29   How does one live like this? Morgan gives a hint. "My ears be open," she told the psychologist, "even when I'm asleep."

30   This was a *child*. Society did nothing to stop these daily depredations upon her. While the legal propriety of the ghetto defense is an important question, the biggest question of all in this story has nothing to do with personal responsibility. It has to do with society's responsibility to poor children like Morgan. What does it say about our society that such a defense was conceived? How can things have come to this pass?

Exercise 2 Discussion and Critical Thinking

1. What writing pattern does Flaherty use in the first four paragraphs that serve as an introduction to her essay?

2. Which sentence in which paragraph contains the definition of "ghetto defense"?

3. What is post traumatic stress disorder (PTSD)?

4. Does Attorney Shellow argue that all poor people living in the ghetto be granted excuses for any crimes they commit? If not, what is she arguing?

5. How is Morgan's case arguably similar to and different from those of battered spouses?

6. How is Morgan's case arguably similar to those of certain Vietnam veterans with PTSD who committed homicide?

7. According to Alex Kotlowitz, how can the inner-city environment be worse than that of a war zone?

8. According to the ghetto defense, where does responsibility lie, with the person or with society?

9. What is your opinion of the ghetto defense?

10. If the ghetto defense has validity, should the concept be extended to anyone who has had extremely violent experiences—"Everyone can point to scars from the past—alcoholic parents, tragic love, etc." (paragraph 24)?

11. Imagine you were a juror judging Morgan's case. How would you have voted and why?

✳ Topics for Essays of Cause and Effect

Reading-Related and Text-Based Topics

"Getting High and Living Low"

1. Using this essay as a model, write about someone you know who has gone through a similar experience.
2. Write about a problem in a larger sense, generalizing about mainly the causes or mainly the effects of drug addiction among young people.

"The Ghetto Made Me Do It"

3. In a reaction write about one or more of the questions posed by the author:

   - If under certain conditions a Vietnam veteran or a battered spouse can use post traumatic stress disorder as a defense, then why cannot a brutalized product of the ghetto such as Felicia Morgan use the same or a similar defense?
   - What is the role of personal responsibility in the commission of a crime, regardless of what the perpetrator has experienced?
   - To what extent is society responsible when a person such as Felicia Morgan grows up under such horrific conditions?

Refer directly to the essay and use quotations from it. Evaluate the author's use of evidence such as examples and comparisons.

Cross-Curricular Topics

4. From a class that you are taking or have taken, select a subject that is especially concerned with causes and effects and develop a topic. Begin by selecting an event, a situation, or a trend in the class content and make a list of the causes and effects; that procedure will almost immediately show you whether you have a topic you can discuss effectively. Class notes and textbooks can provide you with more specific information. If you use textbooks or other materials, give credit or make copies of the sources. Instructors across the campus may have suggestions for studies of cause and effect. Some areas for your search include history, political science, geology, astronomy, psychology, philosophy, sociology, business, real estate, child development, education, fashion merchandising and design, psychiatric technician program, nursing, police science, fire science, nutrition and food, physical education, and restaurant and food-service management.

Career-Related Topics

5. Discuss the effects (benefits) of a particular product or service on the business community, family life, society generally, a specific group (age, income, interest), or an individual.
6. Discuss the needs (thus the cause of development) by individuals, families, or institutions for a particular product or type of product.
7. Discuss the effects of using a certain approach or philosophy in sales, human resources, or customer service.

General Topics

Regard each of the items in the following list as a subject (situation, circumstance, or trend) that has causes and effects. Then determine whether you will concentrate on causes, effects, or a combination. You can probably write a more interesting, well-developed, and therefore successful essay on a topic you can personalize. For example, a discussion about a specific young person who contemplated, attempted, or committed suicide is probably a better topic idea than a general discussion of suicide. If you do not personalize the topic, you will probably have to do some basic research to supply details for development.

8. Attending or completing college
9. Having or getting a job
10. Change in policy or administration
11. Change in coaches, teachers, officeholder(s)
12. Alcoholism
13. Gambling
14. Moving to another country, state, or home
15. Exercise
16. Passing or failing a test or course
17. Popularity of a certain television program or song
18. Early marriage
19. Teenage parenthood

❋ Writer's Guidelines at a Glance: Cause and Effect

1. Determine whether your topic should mainly inform or mainly persuade, and use the right tone for your purpose and audience.
2. Use listing to brainstorm cause-and-effect ideas. This is a useful form:

Causes	Event, Situation, or Trend	Effects

3. Decide whether to concentrate on causes, effects, or a combination of causes and effects. Many short essays will discuss causes and effects but use one as the framework for the piece. A typical basic outline might look like this:

Thesis:

   I. Cause (or Effect) 1
  II. Cause (or Effect) 2
 III. Cause (or Effect) 3

4. Do not conclude that something is an effect merely because it follows something else.
5. Emphasize your main concern(s), causes, effects, or a combination, by repeating key words, such as *cause, reason, effect, result, consequence,* and *outcome.*
6. Causes and effects can be primary or secondary, immediate or remote.
7. The order of causes and effects in your essay may be based on time, space, emphasis, or a combination.

10

Comparison and Contrast: Showing Similarities and Differences

※ Writing Essays of Comparison and Contrast

Comparison and contrast is a method of showing similarities and dissimilarities between subjects. Comparison is concerned with organizing and developing points of similarity; contrast has the same function for dissimilarity. Sometimes a writing assignment may require that you cover only similarities or only dissimilarities. Occasionally, an instructor may ask you to separate one from the other. Usually, you will combine them within the larger design of your essay. For convenience, the term *comparison* is often applied to both comparison and contrast, because both use the same techniques and are usually combined into one operation.

This chapter will help you find topics and choose strategies in writing comparison and contrast.

Generating Topics and Working with the 4 *P*'s

Comparison and contrast is basic to your thinking. In your daily activities, you consider similarities and dissimilarities among persons, things, concepts, political leaders, doctors, friends, instructors, schools, nations, classes, movies, and so on. You naturally turn to comparison and contrast to solve problems and to make decisions in your actions and in your writing. Because you have had so many comparative experiences, finding a topic to write about is likely to be only a matter of choosing from a great number of appealing ideas. Freewriting, brainstorming, and clustering will help you generate

150

topics that are especially workable and appropriate for particular essay assignments.

Many college writing assignments will specify a topic or ask you to choose one from a list. Regardless of the source of your topic, the procedure for developing your ideas by comparison and contrast is the same as the procedure for developing topics of your own choosing. That procedure can be appropriately called the "4 P's": *purpose, points, patterns,* and *presentation.*

Purpose

Are you trying to show relationships (how things are similar and dissimilar) or to prove that one side is better (ranking)?

Let's say you have heard a great deal of discussion about different generations, especially the Baby Boomers and the Generation Xers. Although you could argue that one generation is better than the other, in your quest for understanding, you probably would choose to emphasize relationships. That choice would become a thesis such as this: Although similar in certain ways, the Baby Boomers and the Generation Xers are significantly different.

Points

Next you might brainstorm a list of ideas that could be applied somewhat equally to the two subjects, Baby Boomers and Generation Xers. From the list, you would decide which points have the most potential for discussion. Here is such a list; the most promising points are circled.

(attitudes toward family) (having children, getting married)

music

philosophy (especially optimistic and pessimistic
    tendencies)

fashion

(materialism)

education (both having and wanting)

religion

(attitudes toward careers)

Patterns

You then should decide on the better way to organize your material: subject by subject or point by point. You would use the same information in each pattern, but the organization would be different.

The **subject-by-subject pattern** presents all of one side and then all of the other.

  I. Baby Boomers
     A. Attitude toward careers
     B. Attitude toward family
     C. Materialism
 II. Generation Xers
     A. Attitude toward careers
     B. Attitude toward family
     C. Materialism

The **point-by-point pattern** shows one point in relation to the sides (subjects) one at a time. This is the more common pattern.

   I. Attitude toward careers
      A. Baby Boomers
         1. Details, examples, explanations
         2. Details, examples, explanations
      B. Generation Xers
         1. Details, examples, explanations
         2. Details, examples, explanations
  II. Attitude toward family (same specific support as above)
      A. Baby Boomers
      B. Generation Xers
 III. Materialism (same specific support as above)
      A. Baby Boomers
      B. Generation Xers

Presentation

Here you would use your outline (or cluster list), to begin writing your essay. The Roman numerals in the outline usually indicate topic sentences, and therefore paragraphs. The Arabic numerals (details, examples, explanations) become more specific support.

✳ Practicing Patterns of Comparison and Contrast

Exercise 1 Practicing Patterns

Fill in the blanks in the following outlines to complete the comparisons and contrasts.

Point-by-Point Pattern

John: Before and after marriage

  I. Way of talking (content and manner)

    A. _____

    B. John: After

  II. _____

    A. John: Before

    B. John: After

  III. _____

    A. John: Before

    B. _____

Subject-by-Subject Pattern

Two vans: Nissan Quest and Dodge Caravan (would be more specific if for a particular year)

  I. Quest

    A. Horsepower and gears

    B. _____

    C. Cargo area

  II. Caravan

    A. _____

    B. Safety

    C. _____

❋ Examining Essays of Comparison and Contrast

Student Writer

The Piper Cherokee and the Cessna 172

Brittany Markovic

As a student pilot and a student in a community college, Brittany Markovic leads a life rich in variety and excitement. She rides to school in an automobile, but her mind is in the skies where she flies training aircraft. This comparison-and-contrast assignment provided her with an opportunity to compare and contrast two aircraft often used in training student pilots.

1   When most people think of an airplane, the picture that comes to mind is likely that of a large aircraft such as a Boeing 747. Commercial airlines are what the public is most familiar with, for that is what travelers ordinarily use for long-distance transportation. However, most business handled by airplanes--in fact, about 80 percent of all flights--is done by small planes in what is called general aviation. When a student pilot thinks of an airplane, it is probably a small training plane, the

Subject 1   Cessna 172. Later, the student's attention may turn to another small aircraft, the

Subject 2   Piper Cherokee. Although either can be used

Thesis and purpose   for training, I believe that certain features make the Cessna 172 the better aircraft for the student.

2   For the student at the controls, two key

Topic sentence   characteristics probably come to mind, all

I. Power (Point 1)   related to movement, namely the power for

Point-by-point Pattern   thrust and the landing speed. In all those respects, the two aircraft are similar. The

<table>
<tr><td>A. Piper
Cherokee</td><td>Piper Cherokee must have enough thrust to lift a maximum of 2,350 pounds at takeoff, for which it has 150 horsepower. Then in landing, the Cherokee should come in at</td></tr>
<tr><td>B. Cessna 172</td><td>63 knots. The Cessna 172 has similar ratings: it can lift 2,400 pounds, has 160 horsepower, and lands at a speed between 60 and 70 knots. All of those factors should be considered in relation to the particular flight. The maximum weight matters little in training flights because they are made without extra passengers and baggage. The landing speeds for the two are also about the same and nonconsequential. The only significant matter is found in the power plant, which favors the Cessna 172 by 10 horsepower, small but in some situations crucial.</td></tr>
<tr><td>3
Topic sentence
II. Design
(Point 2)
A. Piper
Cherokee</td><td>That power and speed, of course, must be seen in relation to the design of the aircraft, especially the wing placement. For the Piper Cherokee, the wing is mounted below the cockpit. That design allows for great visibility above the aircraft, which, in turn, is better for observing other aircraft and certain weather conditions. The big problem for the student pilot is that the wing-under arrangement partially blocks the pilot's view of the runway. On the contrary,</td></tr>
<tr><td>B. Cessna 172</td><td>the Cessna 172 features a wing over the fuselage, providing the new pilot with a much appreciated better view of the runway. That design allows the student pilot to more easily master the two most difficult maneuvers: taking off and landing.</td></tr>
<tr><td>4
Topic sentence</td><td>Another point to consider seriously is the fuel system, for the new pilot has enough</td></tr>
</table>

III. Fuel
System
(Point 3)
A. Piper
Cherokee

things to take care of without having to
worry about getting gas to the carburetor. In
the wing-under Piper Cherokee, the tanks are
in the wing, but because the wings are lower
than the engine, the fuel must be pushed to
the engine by a fuel pump, and a fuel pump
may not work. But that possible problem does

B. Cessna 172

not exist in the high-wing Cessna 172. It
also has its gas tank in the wing; however,
because the wing is above the engine, gravity
delivers fuel to the carburetor without need
of a pump. When it comes to airplanes, less
may be more. We all know that gravity is more
reliable than a fuel pump.

5   The first features, the power for thrust
and the landing speed, give the Cessna 172
only a slight edge over the Piper Cherokee.
But the other two factors are decisive.
Better visibility for takeoffs and landings

Cessna 172
better than
Piper
Cherokee

afforded by the high wing and gas delivered
by gravity make the Cessna 172 the better
aircraft for student pilots.

Professional Writer

From B'wood to the 'hood

Ryan J. Smith

Los Angeles Times *researcher, Ryan J. Smith writes about living
on the different sides of town: South Los Angeles and the Westside. His relocation is more than geography. This article was published in the* Los Angeles Times *on February 19, 2006.*

1   When I broke the news to my mother that I was moving from
Brentwood to the 'hood, she immediately began praying for my
protection. When I told friends and colleagues at work of my
planned move toward South L.A., they would pause and whisper, "Oh." Not just any "Oh," mind you, but one freighted with

"Good luck, hope you don't get shot." Strangers thought I was living out the pilgrimage of a young black man who, after a stint on the "outside," was returning to his roots.

2   That couldn't be further from the truth. I was raised by my mother in Culver City before it became "on the Westside." I attended UCLA and settled in Brentwood after graduation. But I needed to escape a bad roommate situation, and my father, separated from my mom, offered me his vacant apartment near Jefferson Park in the Crenshaw district.

3   At first I thought I couldn't survive a move south. I'd tried the 'hood in the early 1990s, when the movie "Malcolm X" came out and my mother decided I needed to know "my people." So I bypassed my usual summer YMCA experience for a camp close to Baldwin Village known as "the Jungles" because of the rampant gang activity nearby. I was called everything in the book. "Why do you talk so white, white boy?" was a frequent question as I was being punched. At night, I cried, but I never told Mom about my camp experiences. One day, though, she coyly smiled and asked, "Black folks sure can be mean, can't they?"

4   Older, more culturally aware and growing ever more desperate to leave Brentwood, I decided to face my childhood demons and take my father up on his offer. The area seemed no different than other urban landscapes in Los Angeles. But adjustments needed to be made. I soon got used to the nighttime "ghettobirds" (helicopters) that plagued the community, and the annoying chime of ice cream trucks that made their neighborhood rounds at midnight. To better fit in, I walked around with a no-nonsense 'hood face—which only made it more obvious that I was not from the neighborhood.

5   "Why did you do that, baby? You have to make sure all your doors are locked!" Aunt Cathy playfully chided me when I told her I didn't regularly lock my car. Note to self: Lock everything! My parents also reminded me of the do's and don'ts when (not if) the police pulled me over. Their advice came in handy one Halloween night when two officers cuffed me and put me in the back of a squad car while they scanned my nonexistent record. Only my embarrassing temptation to blurt out that I grew up on the Westside contained my rage.

6   More discomfiting than the dangers I have to be wary of are the conveniences I miss. I yearn for Jamba Juice and La Salsa—

anything but Jack in the Box or McDonald's. A privilege I took for granted—anytime access to an ATM—ends after 10 p.m. on Crenshaw Boulevard. Nighttime jogging is also out in my new neighborhood. But the Magic Johnson theater at Baldwin Hills Crenshaw Plaza is as good as the Century City cineplex. The smothered chicken and greens at Chef Marilyn's 99-Cents-and-Up Soul Food Express makes me quickly forget the lack of sushi eateries nearby. My neighbors ask how my family and I are doing, a social custom rare on the Westside.

7   I also have become reacquainted with my younger half-brother, who lives nearby. After being shot in a gang altercation, he speaks of his struggle to stay off the streets. His dreams are often tarnished by his quest to avoid jail, drugs and death—a story I hear from too many young men his age.

8   Far more consequential, my color is not what defines me. I'm not seen as a tall black guy, lanky black man or the loud black dude. No woman clutches her purse when she sees me approaching. No walker quickens his step when I am spotted behind him. No one rushes to open a door when I walk down a hall. In my mostly black and Latino neighborhood, my race is no longer a prelude to my being.

9   I don't ache for the conveniences and glamour of my former "home." I drink coffee in Leimert Park. I cruise Crenshaw Boulevard instead of Pacific Coast Highway, enjoying the comforts of my newfound home—doors locked, of course.

Exercise 2 Discussion and Critical Thinking

1. What is Smith's subject of this comparison and contrast?

2. What is his purpose?

3. Does Smith use a point-by-point or a subject-by-subject pattern?

4. What points does he use for his comparison and contrast?

5. In his conclusion (last paragraph), does Smith seem to prefer the Westside or South Los Angeles for a home neighborhood? Discuss.

✳ Topics for Essays of Comparison and Contrast

Reading-Related and Text-Based Topics

"The Piper Cherokee and the Cessna 172"

1. Using Markovic's essay as a model, compare and contrast two other vehicles to show that one is better than the other for particular needs or purposes (everyday driving, certain kinds of work or recreation, making a good impression on peers). Use the Internet or library sources to collect specific information. Give credit to your source(s).

2. Using Markovic's essay as a model, compare any other two products to show that one is better or more useful for a particular need or purpose. Give specific information.

"From B'wood to the 'Hood"

3. If you have lived in two different (culturally, economically, socially) parts of a city and struggled with your own adjustments, write about those experiences. Consider trailer park units and townhouses, company houses and private neighborhoods, barrios and places like Smith's Westside, apartment buildings and private homes, and car or camper living and house living.

   For a text-based essay refer to and quote from the article by Smith to connect his insights with yours, in either agreement or disagreement.

4. Write a two-part response to Smith's essay. Separate your summary from your reaction in which you evaluate his views or relate them to your own experiences. Use quotations and direct references.

Cross-Curricular Topics

5. In the fields of nutritional science and health, compare and contrast two diets, two exercise programs, or two pieces of exercise equipment.

6. Compare and contrast your field of study (or one aspect of it) as it existed some time ago (specify the years) and as it is now. Refer to new developments and discoveries, such as scientific breakthroughs and technological advances.

Career-Related Topics

7. Compare and contrast two products or services, with the purpose of showing that one is better.
8. Compare and contrast two management styles or two working styles.
9. Compare and contrast two career fields to show that one is better for you.
10. Compare and contrast a public school and a business.
11. Compare and contrast an athletic team and a business.

General Topics

The following topics refer to general subjects. Provide specific names and detailed information as you develop your ideas by using the 4 *P*'s (purpose, points, patterns, and presentation).

12. Musical styles
13. Romantic attachments
14. Sitcoms
15. Businesses (selling the same product)
16. Methods of disciplining children
17. Courage and recklessness
18. Relatives
19. Jobs you have held
20. Passive student and active student
21. Weddings
22. Neighborhoods
23. Actors or other performers

❊ Writer's Guidelines at a Glance: Comparison and Contrast

1. Work with the 4 *P*'s:

   - **Purpose:** Decide whether you want to inform (show relationships) or to persuade (show that one side is better).
   - **Points:** Decide which ideas you will apply to each side.
   - **Patterns:** Decide whether to use subject-by-subject or point-by-point organization.

- **Presentation:** Decide to what extent you should develop your ideas. Be sure to use cross-references to make connections and to use examples and details to support your views.

2. Your basic subject-by-subject outline will probably look like this:

  I. Subject 1
     A. Point 1
     B. Point 2
  II. Subject 2
     A. Point 1
     B. Point 2

3. Your basic point-by-point outline will probably look like this:

  I. Point 1
     A. Subject 1
     B. Subject 2
  II. Point 2
     A. Subject 1
     B. Subject 2

11

Definition: Clarifying Terms

※ Writing Essays of Definition

Most definitions are short; they consist of a **synonym** (a word that has the same meaning as the term to be defined), a phrase, or a sentence. For example, we might say that a hypocrite is a person "professing beliefs or virtues he or she does not possess." Terms can also be defined by **etymology,** or word history. *Hypocrite* once meant "actor" (*hypocrites*) in Greek because an actor was pretending to be someone else. We may find this information interesting and revealing, but the history of a word may be of no use because the meaning has changed drastically over the years. Sometimes definitions occupy a paragraph or an entire essay. The short definition is called a **simple definition;** the longer one is known as an **extended definition.**

Techniques for Development

Essays of definition can take many forms. Among the more common techniques for writing an essay of definition are the patterns we have worked with in previous chapters. Consider each of those patterns when you need to write an extended definition. For a particular term, some forms will be more useful than others; use the pattern or patterns that best fulfill your purpose.

Each of the following questions takes a pattern of writing and directs it toward definition.

- **Narration:** Can I tell an anecdote or a story to define this subject (such as *jerk, humanitarian,* or *patriot*)? This form may overlap with description and exemplification.
- **Description:** Can I describe this subject (such as *a whale* or *the moon*)?
- **Exemplification:** Can I give examples of this subject (such as naming individuals, to provide examples of *actors, diplomats,* or *satirists*)?

- **Analysis by division:** Can I divide this subject into parts (for example, the parts of a *heart, cell,* or *carburetor*)?

- **Process analysis:** Can I define this subject (such as *lasagna, tornado, hurricane, blood pressure,* or any number of scientific processes) by describing how to make it or how it occurs? (Common to the methodology of communicating in science, this approach is sometimes called the "operational definition.")

- **Cause and effect:** Can I define this subject (such as *a flood, a drought, a riot,* or *a cancer*) by its causes and effects?

- **Classification:** Can I group this subject (such as kinds of *families, cultures, religions,* or *governments*) into classes?

Subject	Class	Characteristics
A republic	is a form of government	in which power resides in the people (the electorate).

- **Comparison and contrast:** Can I define this subject (such as *extremist* or *patriot*) by explaining what it is similar to and different from? If you are defining *orangutan* to a person who has never heard of one but is familiar with the gorilla, then you could make comparison-and-contrast statements. If you want to define *patriot,* you might want to stress what it is not (the contrast) before you explain what it is: a patriot is not a one-dimensional flag waver, not someone who hates "foreigners" because America is always right and always best.

When you use prewriting strategies to develop ideas for a definition, you can effectively consider all the patterns you have learned by using a modified clustering form. Put a double bubble around the subject to be defined. Then put a single bubble around the patterns and add appropriate words. If a pattern is not relevant to what you are defining, leave it blank. If you want to expand your range of information, you could add a bubble for a simple dictionary definition and another for an etymological definition. The following bubble cluster shows how a term could be defined using different essay patterns.

Order

The organization of your extended definition is likely to be one of emphasis, but it may be space or time, depending on the subject

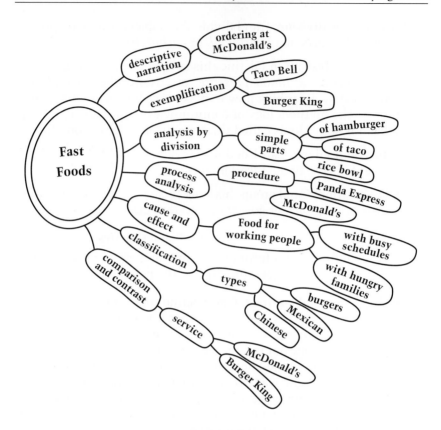

material. You may use just one pattern of development for the over-all sequence. Use the principles of organization discussed in previous chapters.

Introduction and Development

Consider these ways of introducing a definition: with a question, with a statement of what it is not, with a statement of what it originally meant, or with a discussion of why a clear definition is important. You may use a combination of these ways or all of them before you continue with your definition.

Development, whether in the form of sentences for the paragraph or of paragraphs for the essay, is likely to represent one or more of the patterns of narration, description, exposition (with its own sub-divisions), and argumentation.

Whether you personalize a definition depends on your purpose and your audience. Your instructor may ask you to write about a word within the context of your experience or to write about it from a detached, clinical viewpoint.

✳ **Practicing Patterns of Definition**

`Exercise 1` Completing Patterns

Fill in the following double bubble with a term to be defined. You might want to define culturally diverse society, educated person, leader, role model, friend, puppy love, true love, success, *or* intelligence. *Then fill in at least one more bubble on the right for each essay pattern. If the pattern does not apply (that is, if it would not provide useful information for your definition), mark it NA ("not applicable").*

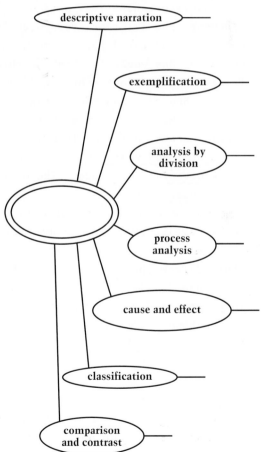

✳ Examining Essays of Definition

Student Writer

Modern Mother

Marie Maxwell

After having read numerous articles about women who are now free to pursue careers, Marie Maxwell reflected on her own situation. Her conclusion is that her situation is more typical than those she has read about. She wishes that were not true.

Background

1   The modern mother, according to dozens of magazine articles, is a super being of incredible organization, patience, wisdom, and grooming. She is never cross with loved ones and never too tired for a game with her children. She wouldn't think of throwing a frozen dinner into the oven and calling it supper. She even has the courage (and the cleaning skills) to own a white carpet. She is a being apart, and I could never quite measure **Thesis** up. <u>I believed that, until I recently decided there were far more women like me than there were Wonder Women</u>.

Contrast

2   The ideal mother featured in the magazines has a lovely home, a handsome husband, and children who at all times appear to have just stepped from the pages of a clothing catalog. Her house is always clean and ready for drop-in guests, and should these guests arrive at supper time, so much the better. <u>My reality is a single-parent home</u>. I have a son who I suspect is <u>colorblind</u>, judging from some of his outfits. Often when I return home from work, I must step carefully to avoid the **Examples** <u>assortment of books, clothes, and toys strewn from one room to the next</u>. Unexpected company

better not show up! As for feeding uninvited
guests--they had better have an invitation if
they expect to be fed.

3   Unlike me, the mothers in the articles
always seem to have glamorous and exciting
jobs. Most of them receive six-figure incomes
and love their jobs (oops!) *careers*. They are
fashion designers, doctors, or managers on
Examples   their way up the corporate ladder. Every
working day is another fascinating challenge
to anticipate. I sigh wistfully as I read, and
I think how dull my secretarial duties are by
Contrast   comparison. I've received two promotions in
eight years--hardly a mercurial rise to the
top. I generally enjoy my job; it pays the
bills and a little bit more, and it has enough
Effects   variety to prevent abysmal boredom. It's just
that I feel somehow shamed by the way I earn
my living after reading an article about the
"new woman."

4   Most magazine writers choose as a subject
a mother who has also returned to school, in
addition to everything else she does. It
depresses me to read that she has usually
earned a 3.80 grade point average, seemingly
effortlessly. Her family cheers her on and
never seems to mind the time that school and
homework demand from her. Even more
disheartening is that her family members
report with pride that she was able to make
those grades without depriving them of their
normal family life. That certainly hasn't been
Contrast   my experience. Algebra, for example, demanded
Example   so much of my time and energy that bitter
words and sarcasm were routine in my
household. When I was married, my husband was

```
       supportive only as long as my classes didn't
       disrupt his life.
   5       Some modern mothers may indeed be just as
       they are described in the magazines, but I
       feel certain that there are many more just
       like me. My wish would be to have a writer
       showcase a woman, if not with feet of clay, at
       least shuffling her way artlessly through a
       cluttered life and, at times, barely coping. I
       might not admire her, but I wouldn't feel
       inadequate, and I'm certain I could identify
       with her. In fact, I think I would like her.
```

Professional Writer

Whose Values?

Janet Pearson

> *Janet Pearson is an editorial writer for* Tulsa World, *a metropolitan newspaper. Notice the care with which she identifies her sources as she deals with the important and difficult question posed in the title.*

1   The terms are all over the newspapers and the airwaves: Family values. Moral values. Traditional values. Judeo-Christian values. Elections are decided based on values. Contentious public battles are fought over values. People are killed every day over values. But what exactly do Americans mean by these terms? How do we view the family and what do we believe about religion in schools? Divorce? Gay marriage? Sex education?

2   If polls are to be believed, there is no one set of traditional American values anymore, if there ever was. The traditional, nuclear American family, along with its accompanying values, has become an elusive species, and taking its place is a new animal. American views about family life and values have become a sometimes-contradictory mishmash, perhaps of necessity. According to a recent poll on religion and the family conducted by Greenberg Quinlan Rosner Research Inc., most Americans

still view the traditional, one-man, one-woman union-for-life as "God's plan" for us all. But at the same time, majorities of Americans don't feel divorce is a sin and about half find cohabitation acceptable.

3   Changing American values probably are a reflection of the new status quo: The latest Census data show only 24 percent of American households have a traditional family structure—mother, father and their children. The Greenberg survey reflected these changes: Sixty-nine percent of respondents were single parents and 19 percent were living with a steady partner. Sixty percent had been married but were not currently married. The surveyors concluded: "We observe a disconnection between attitudes toward the family and lived experiences. . . . Americans in traditional and nontraditional arrangements hold fast to the traditional ideal of marriage and family, where the lucky couples get to live 'happily ever after.' This vision is the aspiration."

4   Though values were deemed a major factor in recent elections, there is not widespread agreement on what the term means. For about a third of those surveyed, the term means honesty and responsibility. About a quarter cited protecting children from sex and violence in the media. Only about 10 percent pointed to abortion or gay marriage and another 10 percent said moral values mean social justice. About 8 percent cited compassion and concern for the sick and needy. "Despite the intense focus on abortion and gay marriage during the election season, most Americans view moral values individualistically, as a set of values that motivate an individual toward acting responsibly and with integrity. They feel that family should remain in the private sphere and tend to balk at the notion that government should be involved in such things as marriage initiatives," surveyors concluded.

5   When it comes to defining the family, Americans also offered a variety of meanings. Nearly two-thirds defined family as their own immediate family unit; only a third of those surveyed defined family in the most traditional sense—married parents and their biological children. Further indication of this broadening definition of family was the affirmative response rate—from 55 to 74 percent, depending on family structure—to this statement: "Love is what makes a family and it doesn't matter if parents

are gay or straight, married or single." The survey found some surprising differences among religious groups. Traditional evangelical parents were more likely than other traditional parents to believe children suffer when the mother has a full-time job, but the evangelicals also were more likely to have two-income households. Religious devoutness, the survey also found "does not make one immune to unsuccessful marriage." Protestants and evangelicals are more likely to get married than other religious groups, but they are no more likely than others to stay married. In fact, about half or more of respondents from all faiths agreed that divorce "is usually the best solution" when a couple can't work out marital problems.

6   There were even more surprises on subjects such as sex education and religion in the classroom. Most parents said they would speak to a teacher if objectionable religious material were presented in their child's classroom. But surprising numbers said they would allow the child to be exposed to the material and then explain why it was wrong. Evangelicals were most inclined to try to have the material removed. Respondents had a "fairly pragmatic view" about sex education, with about 39 percent favoring instruction that focuses on abstinence but also offers instruction about contraception. About 38 percent preferred programs that teach teens how to make responsible decisions about sex. Only 18 percent favored abstinence-only programs.

7   If the shifting beliefs of adult Americans surprise you, wait till you hear views from the younger generation, a majority of whom have had one parent leave the household before the child graduated from high school, and 87 percent of whom had working mothers. A sampling by the same research firm of 892 Generation Y young people—Americans ages 18–24—could portend what is to come for the American family. A shocking 57 percent majority agreed that the "institution of marriage is dying in this country," and an equal number support gay marriage. A similar number also agreed that cohabitation without intent to marry is acceptable. The fact so many of this age group report having gay friends (more than 80 percent know a gay person and a third have a close gay or lesbian friend) explains their acceptance of gay marriage.

8   Of course, views can change with age, so it remains to be seen if the younger generation represents yet another shift in American family life. But history suggests that more than anything, the

American family is adaptable and flexible. There's a good explanation for that: It has to be.

Exercise 2 Discussion and Critical Thinking

1. Pearson begins paragraph 2 with the words "If polls are to be
   believed." Do you believe in polls? To what extent? What about
   the polls referred to in this article?

2. How do you reconcile the statement "Most Americans still
   view the traditional, one-man, one-woman union-for-life as
   'God's plan' for us all" (paragraph 2) with the statement "But
   at the same time, majorities of Americans don't feel divorce
   is a sin and about half find cohabitation acceptable"-
   (paragraph 2)?

3. What does Pearson mean by her statement that "changing
   American values probably are a reflection of the new status
   quo" (paragraph 3)?

4. The author says, "Americans in traditional and nontraditional
   arrangements" believe in the "traditional ideal of marriage
   and family" (paragraph 3). Why is this vision called an
   "aspiration"?

5. How do you rank these ideas as they relate to values: concern
   for the sick and needy, honesty, social justice, compassion,
   abortion, responsibility, protection of children from sex and
   violence in the media, and gay marriage?

6. How do you interpret the following statement? "Traditional
   evangelical parents were more likely than other traditional
   parents to believe children suffer when the mother has a

full-time job, but the evangelicals also were more likely to have two-income households" (paragraph 5).

7. Pearson says, "A shocking 57 percent majority agreed that the 'institution of marriage is dying in this country,' and an equal number support gay marriage. A similar number also agreed that cohabitation without intent to marry is acceptable" (paragraph 7). Should she feel that these figures are shocking? Explain.

8. What possible explanations does Pearson have for the younger generation's views and values?

9. What do the last two sentences mean? "But history suggests that more than anything, the American family is adaptable and flexible. There's a good explanation for that: It has to be."

✳ Topics for Essays of Definition

Reading-Related and Text-Based Topics

"Modern Mother"

1. Using this essay as a model, define one of the following terms (the one you select should apply to you or to people you know): *modern mother, modern father, modern grandmother, modern grandfather, modern wife, modern husband, modern parents, modern kid(s).*

"Whose Values?"

2. Write a two-part response in which you first summarize Pearson's report on values and then, in a separate section, evaluate the views as they stand and seem to be changing. Explain how you feel about the reported changes, especially from generation to generation. Use references and quotations as you discuss whether

current values are good or bad for society. Has reading this article made you reexamine or redefine your own definition of family values?

3. Write a paragraph or an essay of reaction with summary points incorporated. This will be much like the previous topic but will integrate rather than separate the parts.

4. Write an essay in which you define the values of yourself, your family, or any other precisely defined unit.

Cross-Curricular Topics

Define one of the following terms in an essay.

5. History and government: socialism, democracy, patriotism, capitalism, communism
6. Philosophy: existentialism, free will, determinism, ethics, stoicism
7. Education: charter schools, school choice, gifted program, ESL (English as a second language), paired teaching, digital school
8. Music: symphony, sonata, orchestra, tonic systems
9. Health science: autism, circulatory system, respiratory system, thyroid, cancer, herbal remedies, acupuncture
10. Marketing: depression, digitalization, discretionary income, electronic commerce, globalization, marketing channel, free trade, telemarketing, warehouse clubs

Career-Related Topics

11. Define one of the following terms by using the appropriate pattern(s) of development (such as exemplification, cause and effect, descriptive narration, comparison and contrast, analysis by division, process analysis, and classification): *total quality management, quality control, downsizing, outsourcing, business ethics, customer satisfaction, cost effectiveness.*

General Topics

Write an essay of extended definition about one of the following terms:

12. Terrorism
13. Astrology
14. Depression
15. Political correctness
16. "Wannabe" (surfer, gangster, cool, tough guy, athlete, sexy, intellectual, parent, student)

17. A good coach, doctor, clergy, teacher, police officer
18. The Good Life
19. Domestic violence
20. Addiction (perhaps concentrating on one substance or activity such as alcoholism, smoking tobacco, or gambling)
21. A good sport
22. Psychotic (or another psychological term)

✳ Writer's Guidelines at a Glance: Definition

1. Use clustering to consider other patterns of development that may be used to define your term.

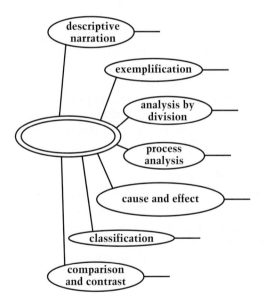

2. The organization of your extended definition is likely to be one of emphasis, but it may be space or time, depending on the subject material. You may use just one pattern of development for the overall organization.
3. Consider these ways of introducing a definition: with a question, with a statement of what it is not, with a statement of what it

originally meant, or with a discussion of why a clear definition is important. You may use a combination of these ways before you continue with your definition.

4. Whether you personalize a definition depends on your purpose and your audience. Your instructor may ask you to write about a word within the context of your own experience or to write about it from a detached, clinical viewpoint.

12

Argument: Writing to Influence

※ Writing Essays of Argument

Persuasion and Argument Defined

Persuasion is a broad term. When we persuade, we try to influence people to think in a certain way or to do something. **Argument** is persuasion on a topic about which reasonable people disagree. Argument involves controversy. Whereas exercising appropriately is probably not controversial because reasonable people do not dispute the idea, an issue such as gun control is controversial. In this chapter we will be concerned mainly with the kind of persuasion that involves argument.

Techniques for Developing Essays of Argument

Statements of argument are informal or formal in design. An opinion column in a newspaper is likely to have little set structure, whereas an argument in college writing is likely to be tightly organized. Nevertheless, the opinion column and the college paper have much in common. Both provide a proposition, which is the main point of the argument, and both provide support, which is the evidence or the reasons that back up the proposition.

For a well-structured college essay, an organization plan is desirable. Consider these elements—background, proposition, qualification of proposition, refutation, and support—when you write an essay of argument, and ask yourself the following questions as you develop your ideas:

- **Background:** What is the historical or social context for this controversial issue?
- **Proposition** (the **thesis** of the essay): What do I want my audience to believe or to do?

176

- **Qualification of proposition:** Can I limit my proposition so that those who disagree cannot easily challenge me with exceptions? If, for example, I am in favor of using animals for scientific experimentation, am I concerned only with medical experiments or with any use, including experiments for the cosmetics industry?
- **Refutation** (taking the opposing view into account, mainly to point out its fundamental weakness): What is the view on the other side, and why is it flawed in reasoning or evidence?
- **Support:** In addition to sound reasoning, can I use appropriate facts, examples, statistics, and opinions of authorities?

Components of Your Essay

The basic form for an essay of argument includes the proposition (the thesis of the essay), the refutation, and the support, although the refutation is often omitted. The support sentences are, in effect, *because* statements; that is, the proposition is valid *because* of the support. Your organization should look something like this:

> *Proposition (thesis):* It is time to pass a national law restricting smoking in public places.
>
> I. Discomfort of the nonsmoker (support 1)
> II. Health of the nonsmoker (support 2)
> III. Cost to the nation (support 3)

Kinds of Evidence

In addition to sound reasoning generally, you can use the following kinds of evidence, or support:

1. **Facts.** Martin Luther King Jr. was killed in Memphis, Tennessee, on April 4, 1968. Because an event that has happened is true and can be verified, this statement about King is a fact. But that James Earl Ray acted alone in killing King is to some a questionable fact. That King was the greatest of all civil rights leaders is also opinion because it cannot be verified.

   Some facts are readily accepted because they are general knowledge—you and your reader know them to be true because they can be or have been verified. Other "facts" are based on personal observation and are reported in various publications but may be false or questionable. You should always be concerned about the reliability of the source for both the information you use and the information used by those with other viewpoints. Still other so-called facts are genuinely debatable because of their complexity or the incompleteness of the knowledge available.

2. **Examples.** You must present a sufficient number of examples, and the examples must be relevant.

3. **Statistics.** Statistics are facts and data of a numerical kind that are classified and tabulated to present significant information about a given subject.

   Avoid presenting a long list of figures; select statistics carefully and relate them to things familiar to your reader. The millions of dollars spent on a war in a single week, for example, become more comprehensible when expressed in terms of what the money would purchase in education, highways, or urban renewal.

   To test the validity of statistics, either yours or your opponent's, ask: Who gathered them? Under what conditions? For what purpose? How are they used?

4. **Evidence from, and opinions of, authorities.** Most readers accept facts from recognized, reliable sources—governmental publications, standard reference works, and books and periodicals published by established firms. In addition, they will accept evidence and opinions from individuals who, because of their knowledge and experience, are recognized as experts.

   In using authoritative sources as proof, keep these points in mind:

- Select authorities who are generally recognized as experts in their field.
- Use authorities who qualify in the field pertinent to your argument.
- Select authorities whose views are not biased.
- Try to use several authorities.
- Identify the authority's credentials clearly in your essay.

✳ Practicing Patterns of Argument

Exercise 1 Completing Patterns

Fill in the blanks in the following outlines with supporting statements for each proposition. Each outline uses this pattern:

Proposition
  I. Support
  II. Support
  III. Support

1. Proposition: Medically assisted suicide for the terminally ill should be illegal.

    I. _____

    II. Better pain management offered

    III. Could be misused by unscrupulous doctors or patients' relatives

2. Proposition: Medically assisted suicide for the terminally ill should be legal.

    I. _____

    II. The expense of care for the terminally ill

    III. The pain and suffering of the dying person

✳ Examining Essays of Argument

Student Writer

Teaching Our Kids to Shoot 'Em Up

Tina Sergio

Tina Sergio's instructor had directed her to write an essay that included ideas from at least three newspaper, magazine, or journal sources. She was to document the ideas she incorporated into the content of her essay and submit photocopies of the works she cited. (See Chapter 13 for MLA style of citation.) A suggested writing topic about the negative effects of media on youth intrigued her. The issue was something that most people of her generation could relate to as they reflected on their childhood: the confusing blur of fact and fantasy in all media but especially in video games and in television cartoons, sitcoms, dramas, and news.

1   Why is it that if video games or television shows contain any type of nudity, many parents become outraged and forbid their

Background   children from involvement; however, when video games and television shows feature shooting and killing, these parents don't bat an eye? What does absorbing all this violence

Authority's
view

teach children? A Surgeon General's special
report has told us that viewing violence on
the media can teach aggressive attitudes and
behaviors, and can desensitize feelings
("Media Violence" 78). It is now a matter of
responsibility for all parties involved.
Parents need to monitor their children's

Proposition
and thesis

consumption of media, and video-game
manufacturers and television networks need to
reduce the amount of violence they display.

2

Authority's
view

Media have become a central force in
children's lives. Educator Donald J. Graff
points out that children now average 35 hours
per week watching television and playing
video games (22). A majority of that time is
spent watching cartoons, and cartoons can
sometimes be more violent than cop shows on
prime-time television. Studies have shown
that prime-time action shows stage three to
five violent acts per hour, whereas violence
in Saturday morning children's programming

Statistics

ranges between 20 and 25 violent acts per
hour (Graff 22). According to psychologist

Authority's
view

Richard Lieberman of Cornell University,
we're seeing an especially high-risk
population for lethal violence in the 10- to
14-year age group because developmentally
their concept of death is still magical.
Children think of death as temporary ("Death
Doesn't Count" 33). For instance, in the

Example

cartoon South Park, there's a character named
Kenny who gets killed in every episode but
always reappears in the next episode.
Although South Park is an adult cartoon, some
parents allow their children to watch it,
mainly because it is a cartoon.

3   Video games are another major contributor to media violence, and kids are spending more and more time playing them. Over the years, video-game action has become much more graphic and grizzly. For example, in the game called **Example**   Doom, the players wander through corridors blasting the guts out of their enemies. What effects do these games have on children when day after day they sit in front of the screens pretending to shoot and kill? Arguably some may lose touch with reality, maybe even lose respect for life. Because video games are not yet rated by the Federal Communications Commission, parents don't realize that video games such as Doom are not meant for children.

4   Unfortunately, violent entertainment survives on television because the audience has been conditioned to expect the harsher realities. The kind of show that contains both of these components--entertainment and violence--is the news. The ratings soar with live coverage of such events as a car chase down a freeway and a man shooting his brains out. It is scary the way the media cover **Example**   tragedies like the massacre at Columbine High School, where two kids kill their classmates and themselves. Surely the nonstop pictures and commentary sometimes give desperate and troubled kids ideas about ways to get attention on network news. It is time for the news media to take some responsibility for what to show and to whom.

5   Violence in the media has become a public-health issue that affects us all. Parents should stop using video games and cartoons as babysitters, and Americans should

<table>
<tr><td>Restated
proposition</td><td>

be a little less hung up on nudity in the
media and a little more worried about the
violence their children are absorbing.
The media and video producers need to
exercise concern and restraint. If all parties
were to show responsibility, legislation
would be unnecessary.

</td></tr>
</table>

Works Cited

"Death Doesn't Count." <u>Newsweek</u> 21 Feb. 1999: 33.
Graff, Donald J. "Violence in the Media."
    <u>Business First</u> 28 Apr. 1997: 22.
"Media Violence." <u>Pediatrics</u> 1 June 1995: 78–79.

Professional Writer

Graffiti: Taking a Closer Look

Christopher Grant

First published as a cover story in the FBI Law Enforcement Bulletin, *this article is included as general-interest material in* InfoTrac, *a data service provider mainly for libraries. It offers a thorough analysis, but it also takes an argumentative position. See how it compares to your own views.*

1   Not long ago, the word *graffiti* conjured images of innocent messages, such as "Tom loves Jane," or "Class of '73." Such simple and innocuous scribblings, although occasionally still seen, have become essentially messages of the past. Most of the graffiti that mars contemporary American landscape—both urban and rural—contains messages of hatred, racism, and gang warfare. Public attitudes toward graffiti tend to fluctuate between indifference and intolerance. On a national level, the criminal justice system has yet to adopt a uniform response to graffiti and the individuals who create this so-called street art. While some jurisdictions combat the problem aggressively, others do very little or nothing at all to punish offenders or to deter the spread of graffiti.

2   To a large degree, society's inability to decide on a focused response to graffiti stems from the nature of the offense. It could be argued that graffiti falls into the grey area between crime and public nuisance. If graffiti is considered in a vacuum, such an argument could appear to have some credence. However, it is unrealistic, and ultimately foolhardy, to view such a public offense in a vacuum. There is a growing consensus in communities around the country that the problem of graffiti, if left unaddressed, creates an environment where other more serious crimes flourish and can quickly degrade once low-crime areas. At a time when law enforcement agencies nationwide are adopting more community-based policing philosophies, administrators are exploring ways to address the basic factors that lead to crime and neighborhood decline. The time has come to take a closer look at graffiti.

Wall Writing

3   **Graffiti** is a general term for wall writing, perhaps humankind's earliest art form. The crude wall writings of prehistoric times and the highly stylized street art of today's inner-city youths share one common feature: Each stems from a basic human need to communicate with others. For youths who may not be able to express themselves through other media, such as prose or music, graffiti represents an easily accessible and effective way to communicate with a large audience. Anyone can obtain a can of spray paint and "make their mark" on a highway overpass or the side of a building.

4   Modern graffiti generally falls into one of three categories— junk graffiti, gang graffiti, and tagging. **Junk graffiti** messages are not gang-related but often involve obscene, racist, or threatening themes. The line separating gang graffiti and tagging has become blurred in recent years. **Tagging,** once seen as a nonviolent alternative to more threatening gang activities, is now considered an entry level offense that can lead to more serious crimes, including burglary and assault. In addition, tagging often results in direct gang affiliation. While all types of graffiti threaten the quality of life in affected areas, tagging and graffiti tied to gang activities represent the most widespread and formidable challenges to communities around the country.

Tagging

5   Tagging as a form of graffiti first appeared in the early 1980s and has grown immensely popular in many parts of the country, in both rural and urban areas. A tagger is someone who adopts a nickname, or tag, and then writes it on as many surfaces as possible, usually in highly visible locations. Although spray paint is the most common medium, taggers—sometimes referred to as "piecers," "writers," and "hip-hop artists"—also may use magic markers or etching tools to create their images.

6   The motivation behind tagging involves fame, artistic expression, power, and rebellion—all integral parts of what has been referred to as the hip-hop culture. Tagging may fill an even deeper void for youths without a strong sense of personal identity. Interviews with taggers reveal a deep desire simply to be known, to create an identity for themselves, and to communicate it to others. The thrill of risktaking also appears to be an underlying motivation for many taggers. While the images taggers create may not necessarily be gang-related, research shows that most taggers hope to join gangs and use tagging as a way to gain the attention of gang members. The more often their monikers appear in different locations, the more publicity they receive. Consequently, a small number of taggers can cause a disproportionate amount of property damage in a community. Tagging messages usually resemble handwriting, but may be difficult, if not impossible, to read. Taggers also have been known to invent their own letters or symbols, often adding to the confusion over the message and the author. . . .

Communication and Territoriality

7   In an article about the increase in area gang violence, a local California newspaper accurately described graffiti as a "crude but effective way for gang members to communicate among themselves, with the community, and with rival gangs." Communication is an important attribute of graffiti that law enforcement and community leaders should understand as they attempt to address the problem. While neighborhood residents and police might see graffiti simply as a blight, gang members and many taggers view it not so much as property damage but as a means to send messages understood within the gang community.

8   The expressive value of graffiti also forms an important com-

ponent of gang territoriality. Gangs, and potential gang members, use graffiti to identify and mark their territory. Although the traditional perception of gang territoriality has been altered by increased mobility via the automobile, research of a noted gang expert indicates that gangs continue to "mark, define, claim, protect, and fight over their turf." In fact, territoriality among rival gangs continues to be a major source of gang violence. Graffiti as a primary form of communication and turf identification plays a direct part in feeding this violence.

True Impact of Graffiti

9   The threat posed by graffiti to neighborhoods and society in general goes much deeper than territorial gang violence. Community leaders need only to consider the reverberating effects of graffiti to understand how a seemingly low-grade misdemeanor can threaten or destroy the quality of life in an entire community. The monetary damages attributed to graffiti speak for themselves. In one year, the City of Los Angeles spent more than $15 million on graffiti eradication. This figure does not include the volunteer time devoted to graffiti cleanup or the estimated millions of dollars spent by private businesses taking care of the problem themselves. In addition, the Southern California Rapid Transit District spent $12 million on graffiti removal during the same year. . . .

10   James Q. Wilson, UCLA criminologist and framer of the "broken windows" theory, states that signs of disorder in society—such as graffiti, abandoned cars, broken windows, and uncollected trash—frighten law-abiding citizens into avoiding public places. Those places are then left to criminals who further deface them, creating a downward spiral in which the fear of crime leads to an increase in criminal activity. The presence of graffiti discourages citizens from shopping or living in affected areas. As established businesses relocate or close, new businesses might be reluctant to move into areas where customers would feel unsafe. As property values decline and law-abiding citizens with resources move, once-thriving neighborhoods can quickly degrade into dangerous places. Thus, the seemingly trivial offense of graffiti ultimately can have devastating consequences for a community.

Response

11   Most experts agree that allowing graffiti to remain visible in a community sends a message that this type of behavior is acceptable to residents. Further, allowing graffiti in an area encourages other offenders to degrade the community with more graffiti or other acts of vandalism. As stated in a newspaper article, ". . . removing graffiti as soon as it appears is the best way to deter further vandalism."

12   Recognizing the serious threat posed by graffiti, a number of communities across the country have developed programs to respond to the problem. The City of Anaheim, California, is considered a leader in developing innovative programs dealing with taggers and the damage they cause. The city developed "Adopt-a-Block" and "Wipeout Graffiti" programs and also established a 24-hour graffiti hotline that encourages residents to report graffiti damage, as well as information about suspects. Information leading to an arrest and conviction can net the caller up to $500. The hotline has proven to be quite successful. To date, callers have received more than $16,500 for information provided about offenders. The courts sentence convicted taggers to perform community service that includes graffiti removal. Anaheim also adopted an antigraffiti ordinance that assigns responsibility for the cost of graffiti removal to taggers, prohibits possession of implements used to create graffiti, and requires merchants to keep aerosol spray cans or other implements used to create graffiti out of direct reach of the general public. . . . To enhance graffiti-related investigations, Orange County, California, uses a forensic scientist specializing in handwriting analysis to help identify chronic offenders. Several other localities in California have passed ordinances calling for convicted taggers to perform up to 80 hours of graffiti removal as part of their sentences.

The Future

13   Although these approaches represent a step in the right direction, they are reactive measures and do little to address the causes of the graffiti problem. the causes lie deep within the roots of social structure; it will require much more than rollers and paint to correct the problem.

14   One of the first steps is to educate the public about graffiti—its meaning and its potential impact on a community. Citizens must understand that this type of behavior cannot be tolerated

because its insidious nature threatens communities from within. To deter new graffiti, young people should be taught that their actions can have far-reaching consequences. Law enforcement agencies may consider augmenting drug- and gang-prevention efforts with lessons on graffiti. Students should be advised that damaging property with graffiti is a serious crime and offenders will be punished. As part of the lesson, instructors also may suggest and encourage alternative methods of self-expression.

Conclusion

15 Like prostitution and illegal gambling, people often view graffiti as a victimless crime. But as communities around the country have learned, there is no such thing as a victimless crime. In fact, crimes that do not produce a single, identifiable victim generally have more impact on the entire community. As a highly visible offense, graffiti represents a particularly menacing threat to the quality of life in a community. The residual effects of reduced property values, lost business, increased gang territoriality, and heightened fear of crime escalate the severity of graffiti-related offenses beyond their impact as visual pollution. Communities that do not develop measures to deter and prevent graffiti now may find themselves confronting more intractable problems in the future.

Exercise 2 Discussion and Critical Thinking

1. Underline the sentence in paragraph 2 that indicates what the author is trying to do.

2. Underline the sentence in paragraph 4 that takes a clear position on graffiti and, therefore, can be called the proposition.

3. Draw vertical lines in the left margin to indicate the sentences in paragraphs 1 and 2 that tie this essay to an audience concerned with law enforcement.

4. According to Grant, what motivates taggers?

5. Why do many gang members do graffiti?

6. What is the "broken window" theory?

7. What form of writing is used in paragraph 10?

8. What is the best way to deter further graffiti?

9. What should be done to deal with the causes of graffiti problems?

10. Does the solution of educating young people about the problems caused by graffiti suggest that the writer has faith in human beings?

11. What parts of this essay do you agree and not agree with? Explain.

12. If you could add one more strong section (or strengthen an existing one), what would it be? Discuss.

✳ Topics for Essays of Argument

Reading-Related and Text-Based Topics

"Teaching Our Kids to Shoot 'Em Up"

1. Use your own examples of the behavior of children and television programming to either support or refute Sergio's views. Include your own experiences if they are relevant.

"Graffiti: Taking a Closer Look"

2. Write a reaction to Grant's definition of graffiti in which you take issue with some of his views. Use quotations from and references to his essay.
3. Write a reaction that is generally in agreement with Grant's view, using your own examples to refer to neighborhoods or towns that have been damaged by graffiti.
4. If you know people who do or have done graffiti, interview them with questions framed around Grant's argument. Then write an essay of argument that accepts or rejects their views.

Cross-Curricular Topics

5. From a class you are taking or have taken, or from your major area of study, select an issue on which thoughtful people may disagree, and write an essay of persuasion or argument. It could be an interpretation of an ambiguous piece of literature for an English class; a position on global warming, public land management, or the Endangered Species Act for a class in ecology; a paper arguing about the effectiveness of a government program in a political-science class; a view on a certain kind of diet in a food-science class; a preference for a particular worldview in a class on philosophy; or an assertion on the proper role of chiropractors as health-care practitioners in a health-science class.

Career-Related Topics

6. Write an essay of argument to convince people that workers in a particular labor dispute should or should not be laid off.
7. Write an essay of argument to convince people that workers in a particular labor dispute should or should not go on strike.

General Topics

Write an essay of argument on one of the following broad subject areas. You will have to limit your focus for an essay of argument. You may modify the topics to fit specific situations.

8. School dress code
9. Homeschooling
10. Sex education
11. Sexual harassment
12. Juvenile justice
13. Endangered-species legislation
14. Advertising tobacco
15. Combating homelessness
16. State-run lotteries
17. Legalizing prostitution
18. Censoring rap or rock music
19. Cost of illegal immigration
20. Installation of local traffic signs
21. Foot patrols by local police
22. Change in (your) college registration procedure
23. Local rapid transit
24. Surveillance by video (on campus, in neighborhoods, or in shopping areas)

25. Zone changes for stores selling liquor
26. Curfew for teenagers
27. Laws keeping known gang members out of parks

✳ Writer's Guidelines at a Glance: Argument

1. Ask yourself the following questions. Then consider which parts of the formal argument you should include in your essay.

   - **Background:** What is the historical or social context for this controversial issue?
   - **Proposition** (the **thesis** of the essay): What do I want my audience to believe or to do?
   - **Qualification of proposition:** Can I limit my proposition so that those who disagree with me cannot easily challenge me with exceptions?
   - **Refutation** (taking the opposing view into account, mainly to point out its fundamental weakness): What is the view on the other side, and why is it flawed in reasoning or evidence?
   - **Support:** In addition to sound reasoning, can I use appropriate facts, examples, statistics, and opinions of authorities?

2. The basic pattern of an essay of argument is likely to be in this form:

   Proposition (thesis)
   I. Support 1
   II. Support 2
   III. Support 3

The Research Paper

✳ The Research Paper Defined

The **research paper** is a long documented essay based on a thorough examination of your topic and supported by your explanations and by both references to and quotations from your sources. The traditional research paper in the style of the Modern Language Association, typically called MLA style, includes a title page (sometimes omitted), a thesis and outline, a documented essay (text), and a list of sources (called "Works Cited," referring to the works used specifically in the essay).

This chapter presents ten steps for writing a research paper. Don't be apprehensive; if you can write an effective essay, you can write an effective research paper. Pick a feasible topic and stay on schedule. (The two main problems for students working on research papers are (1) they select topics that are too broad or too narrow and (2) they fall behind schedule.) The form for documentation is shown in Step 3. Completing a research paper using the following ten steps will give you practice in finding sources in your school library and on the Internet, and it will give you experience in writing a longer, more complicated essay. It will help you master skills so that you can communicate better.

Although specific aims and methods may vary from one research activity to another, most nonexperimental, objective research tasks depend on ten basic steps. See the following explanation and then review the student work for illustration. A complete student final draft follows this discussion.

✳ Ten Steps to Writing a Research Paper

Step 1   Select a Topic

Select a topic and make a scratch outline. Then construct a thesis as you did for writing an essay by choosing what you intend to write

191

about (subject) and by deciding how you will limit or focus your subject (treatment). Your purpose will be either to inform (explain) or to persuade (argue).

- Your topic should interest you and be appropriate in subject and scope for your assignment.
- Your topic should be researchable through library and other relevant sources, such as the Internet. Avoid topics that are too subjective or are so new that good source material is not available.

To write a treatment for your subject, you may need to scan a general discussion of your topic area so that you can consider it in perspective and begin to see the parts or aspects on which you will want to concentrate. Relevant sections of encyclopedias and comprehensive books, such as textbooks, are often useful in establishing the initial overview. At this point, the closer you can come to a well-defined topic with a functional scratch outline of its divisions, the more likely you are to make a smooth, rapid, effective journey through the process. Try to divide your thesis into its functional parts.

Student Example

Tentative thesis: Despite some valid criticism, <u>the zoo as an</u>
subject

<u>institution</u> <u>will probably survive because of its roles in</u>
treatment

<u>entertainment, education, and conservation.</u>

I. Entertainment
  A. Money
  B. Problems
II. Education
  A. General public
  B. Students
III. Conservation
  A. Science
  B. Breeding
IV. Criticism
  A. Pro
  B. Con
V. Zoos of future
  A. Education
  B. Conservation

Step 2   Find Sources

Find sources for your investigation. With your topic and its divisions in mind, use the resources and the electronic databases available in your college library and on the Internet to identify books, articles, and other materials pertaining to your topic. The list of these items, called the **bibliography,** should be prepared on cards in the form appropriate for your assignment (MLA style in this text). Seek different kinds of materials, different types of source information (primary, meaning coming from direct study, participation, observation, involvement; and secondary, meaning coming from indirect means—usually reporting on what others have done, observed, or been involved in), and credible writers (authorities and relatively unbiased, reliable reporters on your topic).

The main parts of the library pertaining to most research papers are the book collection and the periodical collection. Books are arranged on shelves by subject according to the Library of Congress system or the Dewey decimal system. Periodicals, including newspapers, are stored in a variety of ways: in unbound form (very recent editions), in bound form, on microfilm, in databases, and in online computer systems.

Books

Today most academic and municipal libraries provide information about books on online computer terminals, with databases accessible by author, title, subject, or other key words. Usually a printout of sources is available. As with the Internet, selecting key words and their synonyms is crucial to effective use of these online terminals. A combination of words will help you focus your search. In the sample printout on page 194 on the topic *animal?* and *conservation,* the user has keyed in the topic and then clicked to the first title found to check for location and availability.

Printed Material Other Than Books

For the typical college research paper, the main printed nonbook sources are periodicals, such as newspapers, magazines, and journals. Various indexes will provide you with information for finding the source material you need. Depending on the library and the publication, periodicals are listed in indexes printed on paper or in electronic form. The most common index in bound volumes is the *Readers' Guide to Periodical Literature* (now also computerized). It indexes more than 200 popular magazines such as *Time*

```
BOOK - Record 1 of 20 Entries Found                         Brief View
- - - - - - - - - - - - - - - - - - - - - - - - - - - - - - - - - - - - - - - - -
Title:          The atlas of endangered species
Published:      New York : Macmillan : Toronto : Maxwell Macmillan Canada,
                  1991.
Subjects:       Endangered species.
                Endangered plants.
                Nature conservation.
                Rare animals.
                Rare plants.
                Wildlife conservation.
                Environmental protection.
- - - - - - - - - - - - - - - - - - - - - - - - - - - - - + Page 1 of 2 - - - - - - - - - - -
Search Request: K=ANIMAL? AND CONSERVATION           MS<ENTER>=Book catalog
BOOK - Record 1 of 20 Entries Found                         Brief View
- - - - - - - - - - - - - - - - - - - - - - - - - - - - - - - - - - - - - - - - -
Title:          The atlas of endangered species
- - - - - - - - - - - - - - - - - - - - - - - - - - - - - - - - - - - - - - - - -
LOCATION:               CALL NUMBER              STATUS:
REFERENCE SHELVES       333.9516 At65            Not checked out
(Non-Circulating)
```

and *Newsweek,* which means that it is useful for basic research but not for more scholarly studies. The *New York Times* and numerous other metropolitan newspapers are also covered by indexes. For more academic searches, check with a reference librarian for indexes in specific fields such as anthropology or art. Indexes are usually kept in one area of the reference section. The figure on page 195 shows three sample entries from the *Readers' Guide.*

Computerized Indexes and Other Online Services

Computerized indexes, such as *InfoTrac, Periodical Abstracts,* and *Newspaper Abstracts Ondisc,* can be accessed in basically the same way as the online book catalogs, using key words and word combinations. They provide source information, perhaps with printouts. Some indexes include short abstracts (brief summaries) of the individual entries. Some indexes even provide the full text of material. One such index is *LexisNexis,* an online service that can help you find sources and then provide the text of the original source material, all of which can be printed out.

An online essay originally published in, say, *Time* magazine usually will be published without illustrations and in a different format. Therefore, it is important that you give full bibliographical information about your particular source (source citation instructions appear in Step 3).

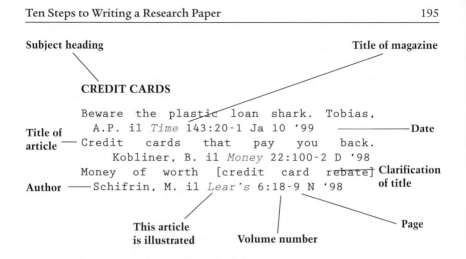

Subject heading   Title of magazine

CREDIT CARDS

Beware the plastic loan shark. Tobias,

Title of   A.P. il *Time* 143:20-1 Ja 10 '99 ——————Date
article —— Credit cards that pay you back.
     Kobliner, B. il *Money* 22:100-2 D '98
    Money of worth [credit card rebate] Clarification
Author ——Schifrin, M. il *Lear's* 6:18-9 N '98   of title

This article   Page
is illustrated   Volume number

    Government publications, pamphlets, and other materials are cataloged in several ways. Procedures for searching all electronic indexes and sources routinely are posted alongside terminals, and librarians are available for further explanations and demonstrations. Many libraries also have pamphlets listing the periodicals they carry, their arrangements with other libraries for sharing or borrowing materials, access to the Internet, databases stored on CD-ROMs, and various online services.

    Search engines, such as Yahoo!, AltaVista, and Google, will yield an abundance of material on your topic. Just key in your subject and choose among sources with discrimination. As with all sources, credibility depends on the expertise of the writer(s). You should ask the following questions: What are the qualifications of the author? What is the reputation of the publication? How reliable is the support? When was the material published?

Step 3   List Sources

List tentative sources in a preliminary bibliography.

Bibliography and Works Cited, MLA Style

You will list source material in two phases of your research paper project: the preliminary bibliography and the Works Cited list.

    When you begin your research, make a list of works that may provide useful information on your topic. At this time, do not stop to make a careful examination and evaluation of each entry, although you should keep in mind that your material usually should come from a variety of sources and that they ideally should be objective, authoritative, and current. For various reasons, some sources may not find their way into your research paper at all. As you read, you may discover that some sources are superficial, poorly researched, overly technical, off the topic, or unavailable. The preliminary bibliography is nothing more than a list of sources to consider and select from.

The sources that you actually use in the paper—meaning those that you refer to by name or quote—become part of the Works Cited list at the end of the final draft.

The MLA research paper form is commonly used for both the preliminary bibliography and the list of works cited. This format is unlike the formats used in catalogs and indexes. The following examples show the difference between printout forms from library files and the MLA research paper forms.

Books

Printout Form

```
Author:        DiSilvestro, Roger L.
Title:         The African elephant: twilight in Eden
Published:     New York: Wiley, ©1991.
```

MLA Research Paper Form

Titles of longer works are either underlined or italicized. Be consistent.

```
DiSilvestro, Roger L. The African Elephant: Twilight in
    Eden. New York: Wiley, 1991.
```

Periodicals

Printout Form

```
Author:        Ormrod, Stefan A.
Title:         Boo for zoos.
Source:        New Scientist v. 145 (Mar. 18 '95) p. 48
```

MLA Research Paper Form

```
Ormrod, Stefan A. "Boo for Zoos." New Scientist 18 Mar.
    1995: 48.
```

Form for Printed Sources

Books

A Book by One Author

> Adeler, Thomas L. <u>In a New York Minute</u>. New York:
>   Harper, 1990.

An Anthology

List the name of the editor, followed by a comma, a space, and "ed."

> Grumet, Robert S., ed. <u>Northeastern Indian Lives</u>.
>   Amherst: U of Massachusetts P, 1996.

Two or More Books by the Same Author

> Walker, Alice. <u>The Color Purple: A Novel</u>. New York:
>   Harcourt, 1982.
> ---. <u>Meridian</u>. New York: Harcourt, 1976.

A Book by Two or More Authors

> Current, Richard Nelson, Marcia Ewing Current, and
>   Louis Fuller. <u>Goddess of Light</u>. Boston:
>   Northeastern UP, 1997.

For four or more authors, use the name of the first author and add *et al.* Alternatively, write out all authors' names.

> Danziger, James N., et al. <u>Computers and Politics: High
>   Technology in American Local Governments</u>. New York:
>   Columbia UP, 1982.

A Book with a Corporate Author

> Detroit Commission on the Renaissance. <u>Toward the
>   Future</u>. Detroit: Wolverine, 1989.

Articles

Article in a Journal

> Butterick, George. "Charles Olson's 'The Kingfishers'
>   and the Poetics of Change." <u>American Poetry</u> 6.2
>   (1989): 28-59.

Article in a Weekly or Biweekly Magazine, Author Unknown

"How the Missiles Help California." <u>Time</u> 1 Apr.
     1996: 45.

Article in a Monthly or Bimonthly Magazine

Fallows, James. "Why Americans Hate the Media."
     <u>Atlantic Monthly</u> Feb. 1996: 45-64.

Newspaper Article

Gregory, Tina. "When All Else Fails." <u>Philadelphia
     Inquirer</u> 2 Apr. 1990: C12.

Editorial

Lewis, Anthony. "Black and White." Editorial. <u>New York
     Times</u> 18 June 1992, natl. ed.: A19.

A Work in an Anthology

Booth, Wayne C. "The Scholar in Society." <u>Introduction
     to Scholarship in Modern Languages and Literatures</u>.
     Ed. Joseph Gibaldi. New York: MLA, 1981. 116-43.

An Article in an Encyclopedia

Cheney, Ralph Holt, "Coffee." <u>Collier's Encyclopedia</u>.
     1993 ed.

Government Publications

United States. Dept. of Transportation. National
     Highway Traffic Safety Admin. <u>Driver Licensing Laws
     Annotated 1980</u>. Washington: GPO, 1980.

Citations from the *Congressional Record* require only a date and
page number.

<u>Cong. Rec.</u> 11 Sept. 1992: 12019-24.

Published Proceedings of a Conference

<u>Proceedings of the Thirty-Fourth Annual International
     Technical Communication Conference</u>. Denver, 10-13
     May 1987. San Diego: Univet, 1987.

Treat particular presentations in the proceedings as you would pieces in a collection.

> Wise, Mary R. "The Main Event Is Desktop Publishing." <u>Proceedings of the Thirty-Fourth International Technical Communication Conference</u>. Denver, 10-13 May 1987. San Diego: Univet, 1987.

A Lecture, Speech, or Address

> Kern, David. "Recent Trends in Occupational Medicine." AMA Convention. Memorial Hospital, Pawtucket, RI. 2 Oct. 1997.

A Personal Interview

> Thomas, Carolyn. Personal interview. 5 Jan. 2000.

Films, Filmstrips, Slide Programs, and Videotapes

> <u>It's a Wonderful Life</u>. Dir. Frank Capra. Perf. James Stewart, Donna Reed, Lionel Barrymore, and Thomas Mitchell. RKO, 1946.

Form for Electronic Sources

Formats vary widely in electronic media because of rapidly changing systems and terms. The information you provide in your bibliography and works cited will inform your reader about such matters as the subject of each source, who has worked on it, where it came from originally, when it was first written and last changed, when you found it, where you found it, and how you found it. Be sure that you give enough information. If you cannot find directions for citing a source, you should identify a form used for similar content as a model, improvise if necessary, and be as consistent as possible.

Do not be intimidated by the length and seeming complexity of the citations. Every part is reasonable and every part is necessary. If you are not certain whether to include some information, you probably should. As you present an orderly sequence of parts in your entries, you must take great care in attending to detail, for a single keystroke can leave your source concealed in cyberspace with no electronic map for your reader.

The examples in this section follow MLA style. More details can be found at <www.mla.org>. Because the nature of electronic sources and references to them are constantly evolving, check each website for changes and updates.

This is the basic form for Internet and Web sources for your bibliography and Works Cited entries:

- Author's (or editor's, compiler's, or translator's) last name, first name, middle initial
- "Title of article or other short work" or <u>Title of Book</u>
- Editor's name (if available)
- Title of electronic journal
- Publication date or date of last revision for any printed version
- Subject of forum or discussion group
- Indication of online posting or Web page
- Page numbers or the numbers of paragraphs or sections
- Name of institution or organization sponsoring or affiliated with the website
- Date of access to the source
- <electronic address or URL>

Online Services—Library and Personal

Library Subscription Services (databases with full texts)

Online library subscription services provide databases mainly of articles in journals, magazines, and newspapers. They are accessed either at a library terminal or by the student's computer. They often include hundreds of publications and enable students to find and print out entire texts rapidly. Although most have complete printed versions, the illustrations are usually omitted, page numbers are changed or not given, and some material may be reformatted. For brief documented papers, instructors sometimes ask their students to include copies of the printouts with the final submission. Content ranges from works intended for the general reader to those written for scholarly purposes. Some are listed as "juried," which means that the selections have been evaluated for credible content by a group of experts in the field. Library online services include ProQuest Direct, LexisNexis, and EBSCOhost.

The basic form is author, title, publication information, service company, library, and date of access. Include the URL of the service in angle brackets if it is available.

```
Fox, Justin. "What in the World Happened to Economics?"
     Fortune 15 Mar. 1999: 90-102. ABI/INFORM Global.
     ProQuest Direct. Regional Community Coll. Lib.,
```

Little Rock. 2 Mar. 1999 <http://www.umi.com/
proquest/>.
Rivenburg, Roy. "The Mean Season." Los Angeles Times
14 July 1995: E-1. NewsBank InfoWeb. Mt. San
Antonio Coll. Lib. Walnut, CA. 8 Sept. 1999.

*Personal Subscription Services (databases with full texts supplied
by companies such as AOL)*

Typically indicate author, title, publication information (if any),
name of service, date of access, and the *Keyword* you used or the
Path (sequence of topics) you followed in locating the source.

"Cloning." BioTech's Life and Science Dictionary.
30 June 1998. Indiana U. America Online. 4 July
1998. Path: Research and Learning; Science;
Biology; Biotechnology Dictionary.
"Tecumseh." Compton's Encyclopedia Online. Vers. 3.0.
1998. America Online, 8 April 2000. Keyword:
Compton's.

Professional Site

MLA on the Web. 25 Nov. 1997. Modern Language Association
of America. 25 Mar. 1998 <http://www.mla.org>.

Personal Site

Hawisher, Gail. Home page. University of Illinois
Urbana-Champaign/The Women, Information Technology,
and Scholarship Colloquium. 18 Mar. 1998 <http://
www.art.uiuc.edu/wits/members/hawisher.html>.

Book

Conrad, Joseph. Lord Jim. London: Blackwoods, 1900.
Oxford Text Archive. 12 July 1993. Oxford University
Computing Services. 20 Feb. 1998 <ftp://ota.ox.ac.
uk/pub/ota/public/english/conrad/lordjim.1924>.
Dickens, Charles. A Christmas Carol. London 1843. The
Electronic Text Center. Ed. David Seaman. Dec. 1997.
U of Virginia Library. 4 Feb. 1998 <http://etext.
lib.virginia.edu/cgibin/browse-mixed?idDicChri&tag--
public&images--images/modeng&data--/lv1/Archive/
eng-parsed>.

Poem

Hampl, Patricia. "Who We Will Love," <u>Woman Before an</u>
<u>Aquarium</u>. Pittsburgh: U of Pittsburgh P, 1978:
27-28. A Poem a Week. Rice University, 13 Mar. 1998
⟨http:// www.ruf.rice.edu/~alisa/Jun24html⟩.

Article in a Journal

Bieder, Robert A. "The Representation of Indian Bodies
in Nineteenth-Century American Anthropology." <u>The</u>
<u>American Indian Quarterly</u> 20.2 (1996). 28 Mar. 1998
⟨http://www.uoknor.edu/aiq/aiq202.html#beider⟩.
Killiam, Rosemary. "Cognitive Dissonance: Should
Twentieth-Century Women Composers Be Grouped with
Foucault's Mad Criminals?" <u>Music Theory Online</u> 3.2
(1997):30 pars.10 May 1997 ⟨http://smt.ucsb.edu/
mto/mtohome.html⟩

Article in a Magazine

Keillor, Garrison. "Why Did They Ever Ban a Book This
Bad?" <u>Salon</u> 13 Oct. 1997. 14 Oct. 1997 ⟨http://
www.salon1999.com/feature/⟩.

Article in an Online Newspaper

"Tornadoes Touch Down in S. Illinois." <u>New York Times</u>
<u>on the Web</u> 16 Apr. 1998. 20 May 1998 ⟨http://
www.nytimes.com/aponline/a/AP-Illinois-Storms
.html⟩.

Newspaper Editorial

"The Proved and the Unproved." Editorial. <u>New York Times</u>
13 July 1997. 13 July 1997 ⟨http://www.nytimes.com/
yr/mo/day/editorial/13sun1.html⟩.

Review

Koeppel, Fredric. "A Look at John Keats." Rev. of
<u>Keats</u>, by Andrew Motion. <u>Nando Times News</u> 16 Apr.
1998. 27 Aug. 1998 ⟨http://www.nando.net/newsroom/
ntn/enter/041698/enter30_20804.html⟩.

Posting to a Discussion List

Inman, James. "Re: Technologist." Online posting. 24
Sept. 1997. Alliance for Computers in Writing. 27
Mar. 1998. ⟨acw-1/unicorn.acs.ttu.edu⟩.

Merrian, Joanne. "Spinoff: Monsterpiece Theatre."
   Online posting. 30 Apr. 1994. Shaksper: The Global
   Electronic Shakespeare Conf. 27 Aug. 1997 <http://
   www.arts.ubc.ca/english/iemls/shak/
   MONSTERP_SPINOFF.txt>.

Gopher

Page, Melvin E. "Brief Citation Guide for Internet
   Sources in History and the Humanities." 20 Feb.
   1996. 9 pp. 7 July 1996 <gopher://h-net.msu.edu/
   00/lists/h-africa/internet-cit>.

Synchronous Communication (MOO, MUD)

Inept_Guest. Discussion of disciplinary politics in
   rhet/ comp. 12 Mar. 1998. LinguaMOO. 12 Mar. 1998
   <telnet: lingua.utdallas.edu8888>.

Scholarly Project

Victorian Women Writers Project. Ed. Perry Willett.
   Apr. 1997. Indiana U. 26 Apr. 1997 <http://
   www.indiana.edu/~letrs/vwwp/>.

CD-ROM

West, Cornel. "The Dilemma of the Black Intellectual."
   Critical Quarterly 29 (1987): 39-52. MLA
   International Bibliography. CD-ROM. SilverPlatter.
   Feb. 1995.
"About Richard III." Cinemania 96. CD-ROM. Redmond:
   Microsoft, 1996.

Article in a Reference Database

"Fresco." Britannica Online. Vers. 97.1.1. Mar. 1997.
   Encyclopaedia Britannica. 29 Mar. 1997 <http://
   www.eb.com:180>.
Atwood, Margaret. "Memento Mori--but First, Carpe
   Diem." Rev. of Toward the End of Time, by John
   Updike. New York Times Book Review 12 Oct. 1997:
   9-10. The New York Times Books on the Web. 1997.
   The New York Times Company. 13 Oct. 1997 <http://
   search.nytimes.com/books/97/10/12/reviews/
   971012.12atwoodt.html>.

Personal E-mail Message

```
Watkins, Jack. "Collaborative Projects." E-mail to
    Gabriel Mendoza. 12 Apr. 2002.
```

Step 4 Take Notes

Take notes in an organized fashion. Resist the temptation to write down everything that interests you. Instead, take notes that pertain to divisions of your topic as stated in your thesis or scratch outline. Locate, read, and take notes on the sources listed in your preliminary bibliography. Some of these sources need to be printed out from electronic databases or from the Internet, some photocopied, and some checked out. Your notes will usually be on cards, with each card indicating key pieces of the information:

A. Division of topic (usually the Roman numeral part of your scratch outline or the divisions of your thesis)
B. Identification of topic (by author's last name or title of piece)
C. Location of material (usually by page number)
D. Text of statement as originally worded (with quotation marks; editorial comments in brackets), summarized or paraphrased (in student's own words, without quotation marks), and statement of relevance of material, if possible

Student Example

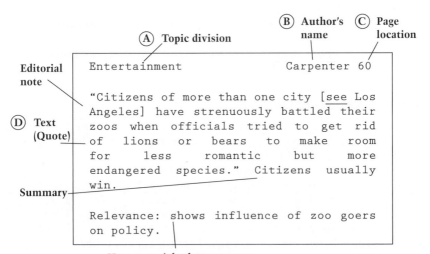

Step 5   Refine Your Thesis and Outline

Refine your thesis statement and outline to reflect more precisely what you intend to write.

Student Example

Thesis: Throughout the world, despite determined opposition, the modern zoo with a new image and compound purpose is taking shape.

    I. Zoos as entertainment
       A. Attendance
       B. Income
       C. Customer preferences
   II. Captive breeding success
       A. National
       B. International
III. Scientific success
       A. Embryo transfers
       B. Artificial insemination
       C. Test-tube fertilization
       D. Storage of eggs, sperm, and tissue
       E. Computer projects
          1. Lab studies
          2. Animal tracking
  IV. Education
       A. Purpose--change attitude
       B. Basic idea--show animals in ecosystem
       C. School applications
   V. Different models of zoos
       A. Zoo/park
       B. Safari park
       C. Regional zoo

Step 6   Write Your First Draft

Referring to your thesis, outline, and note cards keyed to your outline, write the first draft of your research paper. Use the following guidelines to include proper MLA research paper form in documentation.

Plagiarism

Careful attention to the rules of documentation will help you avoid **plagiarism:** the unacknowledged use of someone else's words or ideas. It occurs when a writer omits quotation marks when citing the exact language of a source, fails to revise completely a paraphrased source, or gives no documentation for a quotation or paraphrase. The best way to avoid this problem is to be attentive to the following details.

When you copy a quotation directly into your notes, check to be sure that you have put quotation marks around it. If you forget to include them when you copy, you might omit them in the paper as well.

When you paraphrase, keep in mind that it is not sufficient to change just a few words or rearrange sentence structure. You must completely rewrite the passage. One of the best ways to accomplish this is to read the material you want to paraphrase; then cover the page so that you cannot see it and write down the information as you remember it. Compare your version with the original and make any necessary changes in the note. If you cannot successfully rewrite the passage, quote it instead.

The difference between legitimate and unacceptable paraphrases can be seen in the following examples:

SOURCE

> "What is unmistakably convincing and makes Miller's theatre writing hold is its authenticity in respect to the minutiae of American life. He is a first-rate reporter: he makes the details of his observation palpable."
>
> —Harold Clurman's introduction to *The Portable Arthur Miller*

UNACCEPTABLE PARAPHRASE

> What is truly convincing and makes Arthur Miller's theatrical writing effective is its authenticity. He is an excellent reporter and makes his observation palpable.

LEGITIMATE PARAPHRASE

> The strength of Arthur Miller's dramatic art lies in its faithfulness to the details of the American scene and in its power to bring to life the reality of ordinary experience.

The differences between these two versions of Clurman's statement are enormous. The first writer has made some token changes, substituting a few synonyms (*truly* for *unmistakably*, *excellent* for *first-rate*), deleting part of the first sentence, and combining the two parts of the second sentence into a single clause. Otherwise, this is a word-for-word copy of the original, and if the note were copied into the paper in this form, the writer would be guilty of plagiarism. The second writer has changed the vocabulary of the original passage and completely restructured the sentence so that the only similarity between the note and the source is the ideas.

Check to see that each of your research notes has the correct name and page number so that when you use information from that note in your paper, you will be able to credit it to the right source.

Documentation: Parenthetical References, MLA Style

Although you need not acknowledge a source for generally known information such as the dates of the Civil War or the names of the ships that carried Columbus and his followers to the New World, you must identify the exact source and location of each statement, fact, or original idea you borrow from another person or work.

In the text of the research paper, MLA style requires only a brief parenthetical source reference keyed to a complete bibliographical entry in the list of works cited at the end of the essay. For most parenthetical references, you will need to cite only the author's last name and the number of the page from which the statement or idea was taken, and, if you mention the author's name in the text, the page number alone is sufficient. This format also allows you to include within the parentheses additional information, such as title or volume number, if it is needed for clarity. Documentation for some of the most common types of sources is discussed in the following sections.

References to Articles and Single-Volume Books

Articles and single-volume books are the two types of works you will be referring to most often in your research paper. When citing them, either mention the author's name in the text and note the appropriate page number in parentheses immediately after the citation or acknowledge both name and page number in the parenthetical reference, leaving a space between the two. If punctuation is needed, insert the mark outside the final parenthesis.

- *Author's Name Cited in Text*

    Marya Mannes has defined euthanasia as "the chosen alternative to the prolongation of a steadily waning mind and spirit by machines that will withhold death or to an existence that mocks life" (61).

- *Author's Name Cited in Parentheses*

    Euthanasia has been defined as "the chosen alternative to the prolongation of a steadily waning mind and spirit by machines that will withhold death or to an existence that mocks life" (Mannes 61).

- *Corresponding Bibliographic Entry*

    Mannes, Marya. Last Rights. New York: Morrow, 1973.

References to Works in an Anthology

When referring to a work in an anthology, either cite in the text the author's name and indicate in parentheses the page number in the anthology where the source is located, or acknowledge both name and page reference parenthetically.

- *Author's Name Cited in Text*

    One of the most widely recognized facts about James Joyce, in Lionel Trilling's view, "is his ambivalence toward Ireland, of which the hatred was as relentless as the love was unfailing" (153).

- *Author's Name Cited in Parentheses*

    One of the most widely recognized facts about James Joyce is "his ambivalence toward Ireland, of which the hatred was as relentless as the love was unfailing" (Trilling 153).

- *Corresponding Bibliography Entry*

    Trilling, Lionel. "James Joyce in His Letters." Joyce: A Collection of Critical Essays. Ed. William M. Chace. Englewood Cliffs: Prentice-Hall, 1974.

References to Works of Unknown Authorship

If you borrow information or ideas from an article or a book for which you cannot determine the name of the author, cite the title (the full title if brief; otherwise a shortened version) instead, either in the text of the paper or in parentheses, and include the page reference as well.

- *Title Cited in Text*
  > According to an article titled "Going Back to Booze," surveys have shown that most adult alcoholics began drinking heavily as teenagers (42).

- *Title Cited in Parentheses*
  > Surveys have shown that most adult alcoholics began drinking heavily as teenagers ("Going Back to Booze" 42).

- *Corresponding Bibliographic Entry*
  > "Going Back to Booze." Time 30 Nov. 1999: 41-46.

References to Internet Material

Treat Internet material as you would other material. If the author's name is not available, give the title. Include page and paragraph numbers if they are available; usually they are not.

References in Block Quotations

Quotations longer than four typewritten lines are indented ten spaces or one-half inch without quotation marks, and their references are placed outside end punctuation.

- *Reference Cited After End Punctuation*
  > Implicit in the concept of Strange Loops is the concept of infinity, since what else is a loop but a way of representing an endless process in a finite way? And infinity plays a large role in many of Escher's drawings. Copies of one single theme often fit into each other, forming visual analogues to the canons of Bach. (Hofstadter 15)

- *Corresponding Bibliographic Entry*
  > Hofstadter, Douglas. Gödel, Escher, Bach: An Eternal Golden Braid. New York: Vintage, 1980.

Step 7   Revise Your First Draft

Evaluate your first draft and amend it as needed (perhaps research-ing an area not well covered for additional support material and adding or deleting sections of your outline to reflect the way your paper has grown).

Use the writing-process guidelines as you would in writing any other essay:

- Write and then revise your paper as many times as necessary for coherence, language (usage, tone, and diction), unity, em-phasis, support, and sentences (CLUESS).
- Correct problems in fundamentals such as capitalization, om-missions, punctuation, and spelling (COPS). Before writing the final draft, read your paper aloud to discover any errors or awk-ward sentence structure.

Step 8   Prepare Your Works Cited Page

Using the same form as in the preliminary bibliography, prepare a Works Cited section (a list of works you have referred to or quoted and identified parenthetically in the text).

Step 9   Write Your Final Draft

Write the final version of your research paper with care for effective writing and accurate documentation. The final draft will probably include these parts:

1. Title page (sometimes omitted)
2. Thesis and outline (topical or sentence, as directed)
3. Documented essay (text)
4. List of sources used (Works Cited)

Step 10   Submit Required Materials

Submit your research paper with any preliminary material required by your instructor. Consider using a checklist to make sure that you have fulfilled all requirements. A comprehensive checklist might look like this:

Research Paper Checklist

☐ Title page (sometimes omitted, especially if the outline is not required)
☐ Thesis and outline

☐ Documented essay (text)
___ Approximate total number of words
___ Approximate number of words quoted (Usually, more than 20 percent quoted words would be excessive.)
☐ List of sources used (Works Cited)
___ Number of sources used
☐ Preliminary materials, such as preliminary bibliography, note cards, and rough draft, as required
☐ Double-spaced text, one-inch margins

✳ Student Example

Title page is optional; check with instructor.

ZOOS--AN ENDANGERED SPECIES?

Michael Chung

Professor Lee Brandon

English 1A

9 January 2008

Double-space throughout (thesis and outline section is optional; check with instructor).

Heading for all pages starting on the second page of the paper: last name, one space, page number (small Roman numerals for outline pages, Arabic for paper).	Chung ii

Thesis: Throughout the world, despite determined opposition, the modern zoo with a new image and compound purpose is taking shape.

    I. Zoos as entertainment

        A. Attendance

        B. Income

Align entries in columns

        C. Customer preferences

            1. Favoring certain animals

            2. Favoring animals over education

   II. Pandas for profit

        A. Criticism

        B. Benefits

            1. Money for zoo conservation projects

            2. Money back to natural habitat

  III. Captive breeding success

        A. National

        B. International

   IV. Scientific success

        A. Embryo transfers

        B. Artificial insemination

Chung iii

C. Test-tube fertilization

D. Storage of eggs, sperm, and tissue

   1. For use shortly

   2. Awaiting future development

E. Computer projects

   1. Lab studies

   2. Animal tracking in field

V. Education

A. Purpose--change attitude

B. Basic idea--show animals in ecosystem

C. School applications

   1. Field trips

   2. Sleepovers

   3. Entire high school education in zoo

VI. Different models of zoos

A. Zoo/Park

B. Safari park

C. Regional zoo

VII. Humane treatment of animals

A. Problems without easy solution

   1. Unruly animals

   2. Animals with diseases

Chung iv

       3. Surplus animals

    B. Problems and solutions

       1. Providing better living areas

       2. Engaging animals in natural
          activities

VIII. Response to critics

    A. Acknowledging contributions

    B. Pointing out flaws

       1. Zoos and support for wildlife
          linked

       2. Much habitat destruction
          inevitable and irreversible

½" from top

1" from top   Michael Chung

**Information
here only
if you do not
use a title
page**   Professor Lee Brandon

English 1A

9 January 2008

[Introduction]

Title   Zoos--An Endangered Species?

**Uses
historical
perspective
for intro-
duction**

    Early zoos were usually little more than crude holding pens where animals, often serving dually with circuses, died off and were replaced by a seemingly inexhaustible supply from the wilds. In the first seven decades of the twentieth century, zoos evolved into institutions that offered some education, a little conservation of species, and mostly entertainment. Meanwhile, numerous passionate critics emerged, arguing for animal rights and questioning the effectiveness and appropriateness of zoo

**Basic
thesis idea
as question**   programs. They brought into focus the question, Are zoos necessary?

Chung 2

[Excerpt from body]

Quite aside from the entertainment aspect of zoos is the captive breeding program. In one spectacular captive breeding success in 1992, the National Zoo in Washington, D.C., may have saved the endangered Komodo dragon from extinction by

Statistics successfully incubating thirty eggs. This ten-foot dangerous, ugly creature that resembles a dinosaur numbers only somewhere

Paraphrased around 5,000-8,000 in the wild but soon
material will be represented in numerous zoos

Citation (Browne C1). Now that the incubation process is established, the entire program offers opportunity to restock the Komodo's habitat in Indonesia.

Not all captive breeding projects can end with a reintroduction of the species to the wild. For those species, the zoos have

Quotation turned to science, which has been used in a
introduced
with title variety of ways. In "Preserving the Genetic
and author's Legacies," Karen F. Schmidt says:
name

Zoos are increasingly adapting the latest in human and agricultural

Chung 3

**Block-
indented
quotation,
no quotation
marks**

reproductive technologies to aid

beleaguered species by boosting

their numbers, increasing gene

variety in small populations and

**Words
omitted
(ellipses)**

controlling inbreeding.... Although

still in the early stages, embryo

transfers, artificial insemination

and even test-tube fertilization are

seen by zoologists as having real or

**Citation
after period
for long
quotation**

potential application in conserving

endangered wildlife. (60)

These scientific endeavors began in

the 1970s and now some of them are

commonplace. Female apes are on the pill

and surrogate mother tigers are receiving

**Reference
introduced
with author's
name**

embryos. Schmidt reports that the

Cincinnati Zoo Center for Reproduction of

Endangered Wildlife has frozen "eggs from a

rare female Sumatran rhino that died,

**Blended
paraphrase
and
quotation**

hoping one day to obtain some sperm and

learn how to make test-tube rhino embryos"

**Citation
after quota-
tion marks
for short
quotation**

(60). In many zoos, eggs, sperm, and skin

for DNA storage have been frozen in zoo

labs, awaiting scientific development by

future generations.

Chung 4

[Conclusion]

The zoo of the future will almost surely be a projection of the contemporary model, one that teaches, conserves, explores, experiments, and, yes, even entertains. Captive breeding cannot save thousands of creatures facing extinction but, as Tudge points out, "Captive breeding is not an alternative to habitat protection. Increasingly, however, it is a

Citation, author with two cited sources vital backup" ("Captive Audiences for Future Conservation" 51). Of course, the whole zoo operation must be monitored by those who know, appreciate, and understand animals. Nevertheless, zoos have

Ends with emphasis on thesis demonstrated their value, and they have the potential to continue with their benefits.

Chung 5

Works Cited

Browne, Malcolm W. "They're Back! Komodos Avoid
    Extinction." New York Times 1 Mar. 1994: C1, C4.

Carpenter, Betsy. "Upsetting the Ark." U.S. News &
    World Report 24 Aug. 1992: 57-61.

Cohn, Jeffrey. "Decisions at the Zoo." Bioscience
    Oct. 1992: 654-60.

---. "The New Breeding Ground." National Parks
    Jan./Feb. 1997: 20-26.

Diamond, Jared. "Playing God at the Zoo." Discover
    Mar. 1995: 78-86.

Douglas-Hamilton, Ian, and Oria Douglas-Hamilton.
    Battle for the Elephants. New York: Viking,
    1992.

"Not Endangered." The Economist 13 Apr. 1991: 55-56.

"Project Technology." Malaysian Elephant Satellite
    Tracking Project. 3 May 1995 <http://www.si.edu/
    elephant/eleintro.htm.27Apr.1997>.

Rainey, James. "Dogfight at the Zoo." Los Angeles
    Times. 30 Jan. 2004 <http://www.latimes.com/
    cgi-bin1994.29Apr.1997>.

Schmidt, Karen F. "Preserving the Genetic Legacies."
    U.S. News & World Report 24 Aug. 1992: 60.

Tarpy, Cliff. "New Zoos." <u>National Geographic</u> July
      1993: 6-37.

Tudge, Colin. "Captive Audiences for Future
      Conservation." <u>New Scientist</u> 28 Jan. 1995: 51.

---. <u>Last Animals at the Zoo: How Mass Extinction
      Can Be Stopped</u>. London: Hutchinson, 1991.

☀ Writer's Guidelines at a Glance: The Research Paper

1. The research paper is a long documented essay based on a thorough examination of a topic and supported by explanations and by both references to and quotations from sources.
2. The research paper is no more difficult than other writing assignments if you select a good topic, use a systematic approach, and do not get behind with your work.
3. A systematic approach to writing the research paper involves these ten steps:

   - Select a topic.
   - Find sources.
   - List sources.
   - Take notes.
   - Refine your thesis and outline.
   - Write your first draft.
   - Revise your first draft.
   - Prepare your Works Cited page.
   - Write your final draft.
   - Submit required materials.

4. Your library almost certainly mixes traditional and electronic indexes and sources; you should become familiar with them.
5. MLA style for works cited differs from that used in indexes.
6. You can avoid plagiarism by giving credit when you borrow someone else's words or ideas.

✳ 14

Handbook

This chapter presents rules and examples for grammar, usage, punctuation, and capitalization. One good way to practice basic writing skills is to write your own examples. In working with verb tense, for example, you could write sentences (perhaps similar to the model sentences) in which you apply the appropriate patterns. In working with punctuation, you could write sentences that demonstrate your ability to use different punctuation marks correctly.

✳ Subjects and Verbs

The **subject** is what the sentence is about, and the **verb** indicates what the subject is doing or is being.

Subjects

You can recognize the **simple subject** by asking *Who?* or *What?* causes the action or expresses the state of being found in the verb.

1. The simple subject and the simple verb can be single or compound.

> My *friend* and *I* have much in common.
> My friend *came* and *left* a present.

2. Although the subject usually appears before the verb, it may follow the verb.

> From tiny acorns grow mighty *oaks.*

3. The **command,** or **imperative,** sentence has a "you" as the implied subject, and no stated subject.

> (You) Read the notes.

4. Be careful not to confuse a subject with an object of a preposition.

   The *foreman* [subject] of the *jury* [object of the preposition] directs discussion.

Verbs

Verbs show action or express being in relation to the subject of a sentence.

1. **Action verbs** show movement or accomplishment of an idea or a deed.

   He *dropped* the book. (movement)

   He *read* the book. (accomplishment)

2. ***Being*** verbs indicate existence.

   They *were* concerned.

3. Verbs may appear as single words or as phrases.

   He *led* the charge. (single word)

   She *is leading* the charge. (phrase)

4. Verbs that are joined by a coordinating conjunction such as *and* and *or* are called **compound verbs.**

   She *worked* for twenty-five years and *retired.*

5. Do not confuse verbs with **verbals,** verblike words that function as other parts of speech.

   The bird *singing* [participle acting as an adjective] in the tree is defending its territory.

   Singing [gerund acting as a noun subject] is fun.

   I want *to eat* [infinitive acting as a noun object].

6. Do not confuse **adverbs** such as *never, not,* and *hardly* with verbs; they only modify verbs.

7. Do not overlook a part of the verb that is separated from another in a question.

   Where *had* the defendant *gone* on that fateful night?

✳ Kinds of Sentences

On the basis of number and kinds of clauses, sentences may be classified as simple, compound, complex, and compound-complex.

Clauses

1. A **clause** is a group of words with a subject and a verb that functions as a part or all of a complete sentence. There are two kinds of clauses: independent (main) and dependent (subordinate).
2. An **independent (main) clause** is a group of words with a subject and a verb that can stand alone and make sense. An independent clause expresses a complete thought by itself and can be written as a separate sentence.

> I have the money.

3. A **dependent clause** is a group of words with a subject and a verb that depends on a main clause to give it meaning. The dependent clause functions in the common sentence patterns as a noun, an adjective, or an adverb.

> When I have the money

Kinds of Sentences Defined

Kind	Definition	Example
1. Simple	One independent clause	She did the work well.
2. Compound	Two or more independent clauses	She did the work well, and she was paid well.
3. Complex	One independent clause (underlined) and one or more dependent clauses (italicized)	*Because she did the work well,* she was paid well.
4. Compound-Complex	Two or more independent clauses and one or more dependent clauses	*Because she did the work well,* she was paid well, and she was satisfied.

Punctuation

1. Use a comma before a coordinating conjunction (*for, and, nor, but, or, yet, so*) between two independent clauses.

> The movie was good, *but* the tickets were expensive.

2. Use a comma after a dependent clause (beginning with a subordinating conjunction such as *because, although, when, since,* or *before*) that occurs before the main clause.

> *When the bus arrived,* we quickly boarded.

3. Use a semicolon between two independent clauses in one sentence if there is no coordinating conjunction.

> The bus arrived; we quickly boarded.

4. Use a semicolon before and usually a comma after a conjunctive adverb (such as *however, otherwise, therefore, on the other hand,* and *in fact*), and between two independent clauses (no comma after *then, also, now, thus,* and *soon*).

> The Dodgers have not played well this year; *however,* the Giants have won ten games in a row.

> Spring training went well; *then* the regular baseball season began.

✳ Sentence Problems

Fragments

A correct sentence signals completeness; a **fragment** (a word or group of words without a subject, without a verb, or without both) signals incompleteness—it doesn't make sense. You would expect the speaker or writer of a fragment to say or write more or to rephrase it.

1. A **dependent clause,** which begins with a subordinating word, cannot stand by itself.

> *Because* he left.

> *When* she worked.

> *Although* they slept.

2. A **verbal phrase,** a **prepositional phrase,** and an **appositive phrase** may carry ideas, but each is incomplete because it lacks a subject and a verb.

VERBAL PHRASE	*having studied hard all evening*
SENTENCE	Having studied hard all evening, John decided to retire.
PREPOSITIONAL PHRASE	*in the store*
SENTENCE	She worked in the store.
APPOSITIVE PHRASE	*a successful business*
SENTENCE	Marks Brothers, a successful business, sells clothing.

3. Each complete sentence must have an **independent clause,** meaning a word or a group of words that contains a subject and a verb that can stand alone.

> *He enrolled* for the fall semester.

Comma Splices and Run-Ons

The **comma splice** consists of two independent clauses with only a comma between them.

> *The weather was disappointing,* <u>we canceled the picnic.</u>

A comma by itself cannot join two independent clauses.

The **run-on** differs from the comma splice in only one respect: it has no comma between the independent clauses. Therefore, the run-on is two independent clauses with *nothing* between them.

> *The weather was disappointing* <u>we canceled the picnic.</u>

Independent clauses must be properly connected.

Correct comma splices and run-ons by using a coordinating conjunction, a subordinating conjunction, or a semicolon, or by making each clause a separate sentence.

1. Use a comma and a **coordinating conjunction** (*for, and, nor, but, or, yet, so*).

   We canceled the picnic, *for* the weather was disappointing.

2. Use a **subordinating conjunction** (such as *because, after, that, when, although, since, how, until, unless, before*) to make one clause dependent.

   Because the weather was disappointing, we canceled the picnic.

3. Use a **semicolon** (with or without a conjunctive adverb such as *however, otherwise, therefore, similarly, hence, on the other hand, then, consequently, also, thus*).

   The weather was disappointing; we canceled the picnic.

   The weather was disappointing; *therefore,* we canceled the picnic.

4. Make each clause a separate sentence. For a comma splice, replace the comma with a period, and begin the second sentence (clause) with a capital letter. For a run-on, insert a period between the two independent clauses and begin the second sentence with a capital letter.

   The weather was disappointing. We canceled the picnic.

✷ Sentence Combining

Coordination

If you intend to communicate two equally important and closely related ideas, you certainly will want to place them close together, probably in a **compound sentence** (two or more independent clauses).

1. When you combine two sentences by using a coordinating conjunction, drop the period, change the capital letter to a small letter, and insert a comma before the coordinating conjunction.

    He likes your home. He can visit for only three months.

    He likes your home, *but* he can visit for only three months.

2. When you combine two sentences by using a semicolon, replace the period with a semicolon and change the capital letter to a small letter. If you wish to use a conjunctive adverb, insert it after the semicolon and usually put a comma after it.

    He likes your home; he can visit for only three months.

    He likes your home; *however,* he can visit for only three months.

Subordination

If you have two ideas that are closely related but one is secondary or dependent on the other, you may want to use a complex sentence.

My neighbors are considerate. They never play loud music.

Because my neighbors are considerate, they never play loud music.

1. If the dependent clause comes before the main clause, set it off with a comma.

    Before you dive, be sure there is water in the pool.

2. If the dependent clause comes *after* or *within* the main clause, set it off with a comma only if you use the word *though* or *although,* or if the words are not necessary to convey the basic meaning in the sentence.

    Be sure there is water in the pool *before you dive.*

Coordination and Subordination

At times you may want to show the relationship of three or more ideas within one sentence. If that relationship involves two or more main ideas and one or more supporting ideas, the combination can be stated in a **compound-complex sentence** (two or more independent clauses and one or more dependent clauses).

<u>Before he learned how to operate a computer</u>, <u>he had trouble</u>
        dependent clause   independent clause
<u>with his typewritten assignments</u>, but now <u>he produces clean</u>,
                                    independent clause
<u>attractive material</u>.

Use punctuation consistent with that of the compound and complex sentences.

Other Methods of Combining Ideas

1. Simple sentences can often be combined by using a **prepositional phrase,** a preposition followed by a noun or pronoun object.

   Dolly Parton wrote a song about a coat. The coat had many colors.

   Dolly Parton wrote a song about a coat *of many colors.*

2. To combine simple sentences, use an **appositive,** a noun phrase that immediately follows a noun or pronoun and renames it.

   Susan is the leading scorer on the team. Susan is a quick and strong player.

   Susan, *a quick and strong player,* is the leading scorer on the team.

3. Simple sentences can often be combined by dropping a repeated subject in the second sentence.

   Some items are too damaged for recycling. They must be disposed of.

   Some items are too damaged for recycling and must be disposed of.

4. Sentences can be combined by using a **participial phrase,** a group of words that includes a participle, which is a verblike word that usually ends in *-ing* or *-ed.*

   John rowed smoothly. He reached the shore.

   Rowing smoothly, John reached the shore.

☀ Variety in Sentences

Do not bother to look for formulas in this section. Variety in sentences may be desirable for its own sake, to avoid dullness. However, it is more likely you will revise your essays for reasons that make good sense in the context of what you are writing. The following are some of the variations available to you.

Types

You have learned that all four types of sentences are sound. Your task as a writer is to decide which one to use for a particular thought. That decision may not be made until you revise your composition. Then you can choose on the basis of the relationship of ideas:

> **Simple:** a single idea
>
> **Compound:** two closely related ideas
>
> **Complex:** one idea more important than the other
>
> **Compound-complex:** a combination of compound and complex

These types were all covered earlier in this chapter (p. 225).

Order

You will choose the order of parts and information according to what you want to emphasize. Typically the most emphatic location is at the end of any unit.

Length

Uncluttered and direct, short sentences commonly draw attention. But that focus occurs only when they stand out from longer sentences. Therefore, you would usually avoid a series of short sentences.

Beginnings

A long series of sentences with each beginning containing a subject followed by a verb may become monotonous. Consider beginning sentences in different ways:

> **With a prepositional phrase:** *In the distance* a dog barked.
>
> **With a transitional connective (conjunctive adverb)** such as *then, however,* or *therefore: Then* the game was over.
>
> **With a coordinating conjunction such as *and* or *but:* But** no one moved for three minutes.

With a dependent clause: *Although he wanted a new Corvette,* he settled for a used Ford Taurus.

With an adverb: *Carefully* he removed the thorn from the lion's paw.

✳ Parallel Structure

Parallelism means balancing one structure with another of the same kind—nouns with nouns, verbs with verbs, adjectives (words that can describe nouns) with adjectives, adverbs (words that can describe verbs) with adverbs, and so forth.

> *Men, women,* and *children* [nouns] *enjoy* the show and *return* [verbs] each year.
>
> She fell *in love* and *out of love* [phrases] in a few seconds.
>
> *She fell in love with him,* and *he fell in love with her* [clauses].

1. Faulty parallel structure is awkward and draws unfavorable attention to what is being said.

   > *To talk* with his buddies and *eating* fast foods were his favorite pastimes. (The sentence should read *Talking . . .* and *eating* or *To talk . . .* and *to eat.*)

2. Some words signal parallel structure. All coordinating conjunctions (*for, and, nor, but, or, yet, so*) can give such signals.

   > The weather is hot *and* humid.
   >
   > He purchased a Dodger Dog, *but* I chose Stadium Peanuts.

3. Combination words also signal the need for parallelism or balance. The most common ones are *either/or, neither/nor, not only/but also, both/and,* and *whether/or.*

   > We will *either* win this game *or* go out fighting. (verb following each of the combination words)

✳ Omissions: When Parts Are Missing

Do not omit words that are needed to make your sentences clear and logical. Of the many types of undesirable constructions in which necessary words are omitted, the following are the most common.

1. **Subjects.** Do not omit a necessary subject in a sentence with two verbs.

> ILLOGICAL   The cost of the car was $12,000 but would easily last me through college. (subject of last)
>
> LOGICAL   The cost of the car was $12,000, but the car would easily last me through college.

2. **Verbs.** Do not omit verbs that are needed because of a change in the number of the subject or a change of tense.

> ILLOGICAL   The bushes were trimmed and the grass mowed.
>
> LOGICAL   The bushes were trimmed, and the grass was mowed.
>
> ILLOGICAL   True honesty always has and always will be admired by most people. (tense)
>
> LOGICAL   True honesty always has been and always will be admired by most people.

3. ***That* as a conjunction.** The conjunction *that* should not be omitted from a dependent clause if there is danger of misreading the sentence.

> MISLEADING   We believed Eric, if not stopped, would hurt himself.
>
> CLEAR   We believed that Eric, if not stopped, would hurt himself.

4. **Prepositions.** Do not omit prepositions in idiomatic phrases, in expressions of time, and in parallel phrases.

> ILLOGICAL   Weekends the campus is deserted. (time)
>
> LOGICAL   During weekends the campus is deserted.
>
> ILLOGICAL   I have neither love nor patience with untrained dogs. (parallel phrases)
>
> LOGICAL   I have neither love for nor patience with untrained dogs.
>
> ILLOGICAL   Glenda's illness was something we heard only after her recovery. (preposition omitted)
>
> LOGICAL   Glenda's illness was something we heard about only after her recovery.

✳ Verbs

The twelve verb tenses are shown in this section. The irregular verb *drive* is used as the example. (See pp. 235–236 for a list of irregular verbs.)

Simple Tenses

Present

I, we, you, they *drive.*
He, she, it *drives.*

May imply
a continuation from
past to future

Past

I, we, you, he, she, it, they *drove.*

Future

I, we, you, he, she, it,
they *will drive.*

Perfect Tenses

Present Perfect

I, we, you, they *have driven.*
He, she, it *has driven.*

Completed recently
in the past, may con-
tinue to the present

Past Perfect

I, we, you, he, she, it, they *had driven.*

Completed prior to a
specific time in the
past

Future Perfect

I, we, you, he, she, it, they *will have
driven.*

Will occur at a time
prior to a specific
time in the future

Progressive Tenses

Present Progressive

I *am driving.*
He, she, it *is driving.*
We, you, they *are driving.*

In progress now

Past Progressive

I, he, she, it *was driving.*
We, you, they *were driving.*

In progress in the
past

Future Progressive

I, we, you, he, she, it, they *will be
driving.*

In progress in the
future

Perfect Progressive Tenses

Present Perfect Progressive

I, we, you, they *have been driving.*
He, she, it *has been driving.*

In progress up to now

Past Perfect Progressive

I, we, you, he, she, it, they *had been driving.*

In progress before another event in the past

Future Perfect Progressive

I, we, you, he, she, it, they *will have been driving.*

In progress before another event in the future

Past Participles

The past participle uses the helping verbs *has, have,* or *had* along with the past tense of the verb. For regular verbs, whose past tense ends in *-ed,* the past participle form of the verb is the same as the past tense.

Following is a list of some common regular verbs, showing the base form, the past tense, and the past participle. (The base form can also be used with such helping verbs as *can, could, do, does, did, may, might, must, shall, should, will,* and *would.*)

Regular Verbs

Base Form (Present)	Past	Past Participle
ask	asked	asked
answer	answered	answered
cry	cried	cried
decide	decided	decided
dive	dived (dove)	dived
drag	dragged	dragged
finish	finished	finished
happen	happened	happened
learn	learned	learned
like	liked	liked
love	loved	loved
need	needed	needed
open	opened	opened

Base Form (Present)	Past	Past Participle
start	started	started
suppose	supposed	supposed
walk	walked	walked
want	wanted	wanted

Whereas **regular verbs** are predictable—having an *-ed* ending for past and past-participle forms—**irregular verbs,** as the term suggests, follow no definite pattern.

Following is a list of some common irregular verbs, showing the base form (present), the past tense, and the past participle.

Irregular Verbs

Base Form (Present)	Past	Past Participle
arise	arose	arisen
awake	awoke (awaked)	awaked
be	was, were	been
become	became	become
begin	began	begun
bend	bent	bent
blow	blew	blown
break	broke	broken
bring	brought	brought
buy	bought	bought
catch	caught	caught
choose	chose	chosen
cling	clung	clung
come	came	come
creep	crept	crept
deal	dealt	dealt
do	did	done
drink	drank	drunk
drive	drove	driven
eat	ate	eaten
feel	felt	felt
fight	fought	fought
fling	flung	flung
fly	flew	flown
forget	forgot	forgotten
freeze	froze	frozen
get	got	got (gotten)

(continued)

Base Form (Present)	Past	Past Participle
go	went	gone
grow	grew	grown
have	had	had
know	knew	known
lead	led	led
leave	left	left
lose	lost	lost
mean	meant	meant
read	read	read
ride	rode	ridden
ring	rang	rung
see	saw	seen
shine	shone (shined)	shone (shined)
shoot	shot	shot
sing	sang	sung
sink	sank	sunk
sleep	slept	slept
slink	slunk	slunk
speak	spoke	spoken
spend	spent	spent
steal	stole	stolen
stink	stank (stunk)	stunk
sweep	swept	swept
swim	swam	swum
swing	swung	swung
take	took	taken
teach	taught	taught
tear	tore	torn
think	thought	thought
throw	threw	thrown
wake	woke (waked)	woken (waked)
weep	wept	wept
write	wrote	written

"Problem" Verbs

The following pairs of verbs are especially troublesome and confusing: *lie* and *lay, sit* and *set,* and *rise* and *raise.* One way to tell them apart is to remember which word in each pair takes a direct object. A direct object answers the question *whom* or *what* in connection with a verb. The words *lay, raise,* and *set* take a direct object.

He *raised* the window. (He *raised* what?)

Lie, rise, and *sit,* however, cannot take a direct object. We cannot say, for example, "He rose the window." In the following examples, the italicized words are objects.

Present Tense	Meaning	Past Tense	Past Participle	Example
lie	to rest	lay	lain	I lay down to rest.
lay	to place something	laid	laid	We laid the *books* on the table.
rise	to go up	rose	risen	The smoke rose quickly.
raise	to lift	raised	raised	She raised the *question.*
sit	to rest	sat	sat	He sat in the chair.
set	to place something	set	set	They set the *basket* on the floor.

Verb Tense

Verb tense is a word form indicating time. The rules about selecting a tense for certain kinds of writing are flexible. You should be consistent, however, changing tense only for a good reason.

Usually you should select the present tense to write about literature.

Moby Dick *is* a famous white whale.

Select the past tense to write about yourself (usually) or something historical (always).

I *was* eighteen when I *decided* I *was* ready for independence.

Subject-Verb Agreement

The basic principle of **subject-verb agreement** is that if the subject is singular, the verb should be singular, and if the subject is plural, the verb should be plural.

The *advantages* of that shoe *are* obvious.

There *are* many *reasons* for his poor work.

The *coach,* along with the players, *protests* the decision.

The *price* of those shoes *is* too high.

Voice

The **active voice** (subject, active verb, and object) is usually pre-ferred over the **passive voice** (subject as the receiver of action, with doer unstated or at the end of a prepositional phrase).

ACTIVE   She read the book.

PASSIVE   The book was read by her.

※ Pronouns

A **pronoun** is a word that is used in place of a noun. **Case** is the form a pronoun takes as it fills a position in a sentence.

1. **Subjective pronouns** are *I, he,* and *she* (singular), and *we* and *they* (plural). *Who* can be either singular or plural.
   Subjective case pronouns can fill subject positions in a sentence.

   We dance in the park.

   It was *she* who spoke. (referring back to and meaning the same as the subject)

2. **Objective pronouns** are *me, him,* and *her* (singular); and *us* and *them* (plural). *Whom* can be either singular or plural.
   Objective case pronouns fill object positions.

   We saw *her* in the library. (object of verb)

   They gave the results to *us*—Judy and *me.* (object of a preposition)

3. Three techniques are useful for deciding what pronoun case to use.
   a. If you have a compound element (such as a subject or an ob-ject of a preposition), consider only the pronoun part.

   They will visit Jim and (I, me). (*Consider:* They will visit *me.*)

   b. If the next important word after *who* or *whom* in a state-ment is a noun or pronoun, the word choice will be *whom;* otherwise, it will be *who.* Disregard qualifier clauses such as *It seems* and *I feel.*

   The person *who* works hardest will win.

   The person *whom* judges like will win.

The person *who,* we think, worked hardest won. (ignoring the qualifier clause)

c. *Let's* is made up of the words *let* and *us* and means "you *let us*"; therefore, when you select a pronoun to follow it, consider the two original words and select another object word—*me.*

Let's you and *me* go to town.

4. A pronoun agrees with its antecedent in person, number, and gender.
   a. Avoid needless shifting in person, which means shifting in point of view, such as from *I* to *you.*

      INCORRECT *I* tried but *you* couldn't persuade her to return.

      CORRECT *I* tried but *I* couldn't persuade her to return.

   b. Most problems with pronoun-antecedent agreement involve number. The principles are simple: If the antecedent (the word the pronoun refers back to) is singular, use a singular pronoun. If the antecedent is plural, use a plural pronoun.

      Jim forgot *his* notebook.

      Many students cast *their* votes today.

      Someone lost *his* or *her* [not *their*] book.

   c. The pronoun should agree with its antecedent in gender if the gender of the antecedent is specific. Masculine and feminine pronouns are gender-specific: *he, him, she,* and *her.* Others are neuter: *I, we, me, us, it, they, them, who, whom, that,* and *which.* The words *who* and *whom* refer to people. *That* can refer to ideas, things, and people, but usually not to people. *Which* refers to ideas and things, but never to people. To avoid a perceived sex bias, most writers and speakers prefer to use *he or she* or *his or her* instead of just *he* or *his;* however, many writers simply make antecedents plural.

      Everyone should work until *he or she* drops.

      People should work until *they* drop.

☀ Adjectives and Adverbs

1. **Adjectives** modify (describe) nouns and pronouns and answer the questions *Which one? What kind?* and *How many?*
2. **Adverbs** modify verbs, adjectives, or other adverbs and answer the questions *How? Where? When?* and *To what degree?* Most words ending in *-ly* are adverbs.
3. If you settle for a common word such as *good* or a slang word such as *neat* to characterize something you like, you will be limiting your communication. The more precise the word, the better the communication. Keep in mind, however, that anything can be overdone; therefore, use adjectives and adverbs wisely and economically.
4. For making comparisons, most adjectives and adverbs have three different forms: the positive (one), the comparative (two), and the superlative (three or more).
   a. Adjectives
      - Add *-er* to short adjectives (one or two syllables) to rank units of two.

         Julian is *kinder* than Sam.

      - Add *-est* to short adjectives (one or two syllables) to rank units of more than two.

         Of the fifty people I know, Julian is the *kindest.*

      - Add the word *more* before long adjectives to rank units of two.

         My hometown is *more beautiful* than yours.

      - Add the word *most* before long adjectives to rank units of three or more.

         My hometown is the *most beautiful* in all America.

      - Some adjectives are irregular in the way they change to show comparison: *good, better, best; bad, worse, worst.*
   b. Adverbs
      For most adverbs, use the word *more* before the comparative form (two) and the word *most* before the superlative form (three or more).

         Jim performed *skillfully.* (modifier)

         Joan performed *more skillfully* than Sam. (comparative modifier)

But Susan performed *most skillfully* of all. (superlative modifier)

5. Avoid double negatives. Words such as *no, not, none, nothing, never, hardly, barely,* and *scarcely* should not be combined.

INCORRECT   I *don't* have *no* time for recreation.

CORRECT   I have *no* time for recreation.

CORRECT   I *don't* have time for recreation.

6. Do not confuse adjectives (*bad*) with adverbs (*badly*).

7. A modifier that gives information but doesn't refer to a word or group of words already in the sentence is called a **dangling modifier.**

DANGLING   *Walking down the street,* a snake startled me.

CORRECT   *Walking down the street,* I was startled by a snake.

8. A modifier that is placed so that it modifies the wrong word or words is called a **misplaced modifier.**

MISPLACED   The sick man went to a doctor *with a high fever.*

CORRECT   The sick man *with a high fever* went to a doctor.

✳ Avoiding Wordy Phrases

Certain phrases clutter sentences, consuming our time in writing and our readers' time in reading. Watch for wordy phrases as you revise and edit.

WORDY   *Due to the fact that* he was unemployed, he had to use public transportation.

CONCISE   *Because* he was unemployed, he had to use public transportation.

WORDY   *Deep down inside* he believed that the Red Sox would win.

CONCISE   He believed that the Red Sox would win.

Wordy	**Concise**
at the present time	now
basic essentials	essentials

blend together	blend
it is clear that	(delete)
due to the fact that	because
for the reason that	because
I felt inside	I felt
in most cases	usually
as a matter of fact	in fact
in the event that	if
until such time as	until
I personally feel	I feel
in this modern world	today
in order to	to
most of the people	most people
along the lines of	like
past experience	experience
at that point in time	then
in the final analysis	finally
in the near future	soon
have a need for	need
in this day and age	now

✳ Punctuation

1. The three marks of end punctuation are periods, question marks, and exclamation points.
    a. Periods
       Place a period after a statement.
       Place a period after common abbreviations.
       Use an ellipsis—three periods within a sentence and four periods at the end of a sentence—to indicate that words have been omitted from quoted material.

          He stopped walking and the buildings . . . rose up out of the misty courtroom. . . . (James Thurber, "The Secret Life of Walter Mitty")

    b. Question marks
       Place a question mark at the end of a direct question.
       Use a single question mark in sentence constructions that contain a double question—that is, a quoted question within a question.

Mr. Martin said, "Did he say, 'Are we going?'"

Do *not* use a question mark after an indirect (reported) question.

She asked me what caused the slide.

c. Exclamation points
Place an exclamation point after a word or group of words that expresses strong feeling.
Do not overwork the exclamation point. Do not use double exclamation points.

2. The comma is used essentially to separate and to set off sentence elements.

a. Use a comma to separate main clauses joined by one of the coordinating conjunctions—*for, and, nor, but, or, yet, so.*

We went to the game, *but* it was canceled.

b. Use a comma after introductory dependent clauses and long introductory phrases (generally, four or more words is considered long).

Before she and I arrived, the meeting was called to order.

c. Use a comma to separate words, phrases, and clauses in a series.

He ran *down the street, across the park,* and *into the arms* of his father.

d. Use a comma to separate coordinate adjectives not joined by *and* that modify the same noun.

I need a *sturdy, reliable* truck.

e. Use a comma to separate sentence elements that might be misread.

Inside, the dog scratched his fleas.

f. Use commas to set off (enclose) nonessential (unnecessary for meaning of the sentence) words, phrases, and clauses.

Maria, *who studied hard,* will pass.

g. Use commas to set off parenthetical elements such as mild interjections (*oh, well, yes, no,* and others), most conjunctive adverbs (*however, otherwise, therefore, similarly, hence, on the other hand*, and *consequently*, but not *then, thus, soon, now*, and *also*), quotation indicators, and special abbreviations (*etc., i.e., e.g.*, and others).

> *Oh*, what a silly question! (mild interjection)
>
> It is necessary, *of course*, to leave now. (sentence modifier)
>
> We left early; *however*, we missed the train anyway. (conjunctive adverb)
>
> "When I was in school," *he said*, "I read widely." (quotation indicators)
>
> Books, papers, pens, *etc.*, were scattered on the floor. (The abbreviation *etc.*, however, should be used sparingly.)

h. Use commas to set off nouns used as direct address.

> Play it again, *Sam.*

i. Use commas to separate the numbers in a date.

> June *4, 1965*, is a day I will remember.

j. Use commas to separate the city from the state. No comma is used between the state and the Zip code.

> Walnut, CA 91789

k. Use a comma following the salutation and the complementary closing in a letter (but in a business letter, use a colon after the salutation).

> Dear John,
> Sincerely,

l. Use a comma in numbers to set off groups of three digits. However, omit the comma in dates and in long serial numbers, page numbers, and street numbers.

> The total assets were *$2,000,000*.
>
> I was born in 1989.

3. The semicolon indicates a stronger division than the comma. It is used principally to separate independent clauses within a sentence.
   a. Use a semicolon to separate independent clauses not joined by a coordinating conjunction.

   > You must buy that car today; tomorrow will be too late.

b. Use a semicolon between two independent clauses joined by a conjunctive adverb (such as *however, otherwise, therefore, similarly, hence, on the other hand, then, consequently, accordingly, thus*).

> It was very late; *therefore,* I remained at the hotel.

4. Quotation marks bring special attention to words.

a. Quotation marks are used principally to set off direct quotations. A direct quotation consists of material taken from the written work or the direct speech of others; it is set off by double quotation marks. Single quotation marks are used to set off a quotation within a quotation.

> He said, "I don't remember if she said, 'Wait for me.'"

b. Use double quotation marks to set off titles of shorter pieces of writing such as magazine articles, essays, short stories, short poems, one-act plays, chapters in books, songs, and separate pieces of writing published as part of a larger work.

> The book *Literature: Structure, Sound, and Sense* contains a deeply moving poem titled "On Wenlock Edge."
>
> Have you read "The Use of Force," a short story by William Carlos Williams?
>
> My favorite Elvis song is "Don't Be Cruel."

c. Punctuation with quotation marks follows definite rules.

- A period or a comma is always placed *inside* the quotation marks.

  > Our assignment for Monday was to read Poe's "The Raven."
  >
  > "I will read you the story," he said. "It is a good one."

- A semicolon or a colon is always placed *outside* the quotation marks.

  > He read Robert Frost's poem "Design"; then he gave the examination.

- A question mark, an exclamation point, or a dash is placed *outside* the quotation marks when it applies to the entire sentence and *inside* the quotation marks when it applies to the material in quotation marks.

He asked, "Am I responsible for everything?" (quoted question within a statement)

Did you hear him say, "I have the answer"? (statement within a question)

Did she say, "Are we ready?" (question within a question)

She shouted, "Impossible!" (exclamation)

"I hope—that is, I—" he began. (dash)

5. Italics (slanting type) is used to call special attention to certain words or groups of words. In handwriting, such words are underlined.

   a. Italicize (underline) foreign words and phrases that are still listed in the dictionary as foreign.

      c'est la vie   Weltschmerz

   b. Italicize (underline) titles of books (except the Bible); long poems; plays; magazines; motion pictures; musical compositions; newspapers; works of art; names of aircraft; ships; and letters, figures, and words referred to by their own name.

      War and Peace   Apollo 12   leaving *o* out of *sophomore*

6. The dash is used when a stronger break than the comma is needed. It can also be used to indicate a break in the flow of thought and to emphasize words (less formal than the colon in this situation).

   Here is the true reason—but maybe you don't care.

   English, French, history—these are the subjects I like.

7. The colon is a formal mark of punctuation used chiefly to introduce something that is to follow, such as a list, a quotation, or an explanation.

   These cars are my favorites: Cadillac, Chevrolet, Buick, Oldsmobile, and Pontiac.

8. Parentheses are used to set off material that is of relatively little importance to the main thought of the sentence. Such material—numbers that designate items in a series, figures, supplementary material, and sometimes explanatory details— merely amplifies the main thought.

   The years of the era (1961–1973) were full of action.

Her husband (she had been married only a year) died last week.

9. Brackets are used within a quotation to set off editorial additions or corrections made by the person who is quoting.

> Churchill said: "It [the Yalta Agreement] contained many mistakes."

10. The apostrophe is used with nouns and indefinite pronouns to show possession; to show the omission of letters and figures in contractions; and to form the plurals of letters, figures, and words referred to as words.

> man's coat   girls' clothes
> *you're* (contraction of *you are*)   five *and*'s

11. The hyphen brings two or more words together into a single compound word. Correct hyphenation, therefore, is essentially a spelling problem rather than one of punctuation. Because the hyphen is not used with any degree of consistency, consult your dictionary for current usage. Study the following as a beginning guide.

   a. Use a hyphen to separate the parts of many compound words.

   > about-face   go-between

   b. Use a hyphen between prefixes and proper names.

   > all-American   mid-November

   c. Use a hyphen to join two or more words used as a single adjective modifier before a noun.

   > first-class service   hard-fought game
   > sad-looking mother

   d. Use a hyphen with spelled-out compound numbers up to ninety-nine and with fractions.

   > twenty-six   two-thirds

Note: Dates, street addresses, numbers requiring more than two words, chapter and page numbers, time followed directly by *a.m.* or *p.m.*, and figures after a dollar sign or before measurement abbreviations are usually written as figures, not words.

☀ Capitalization

In English, there are many conventions concerning the use of capital letters. Here are some of them.

1. Capitalize the first word of a sentence.
2. Capitalize proper nouns and adjectives derived from proper nouns.

   - Names of persons
     Edward Jones

   - Adjectives derived from proper nouns
     a Shakespearean sonnet   an English class

   - Countries, nationalities, races, and languages
     Germany   English   Spanish   Chinese

   - States, regions, localities, and other geographical divisions
     California   the Far East   the South

   - Oceans, lakes, mountains, deserts, streets, and parks
     Lake Superior   Sahara Desert   Fifth Avenue

   - Educational institutions, schools, and courses
     Santa Ana College   Joe Hill School
     Rowland High School   Math 3

   - Organizations and their members
     Boston Red Sox   Audubon Society   Boy Scouts

   - Corporations, governmental agencies or departments, and trade names
     U.S. Steel Corporation   Treasury Department
     White Memorial Library   Coke

   - Calendar references such as holidays, days of the week, and months
     Easter   Tuesday   January

   - Historic eras, periods, documents, and laws
     First Crusade   Romantic Age
     Declaration of Independence   Geneva Convention

3. Capitalize words denoting family relationships when they are used before a name or substituted for a name.

He walked with his nephew and Aunt Grace.

but

He walked with his nephew and his aunt.

Grandmother and Mother are away on vacation.

but

My grandmother and my mother are away on vacation.

4. Capitalize abbreviations after names.

Henry White Jr.   William Green, M.D.

5. Capitalize titles of essays, books, plays, movies, poems, magazines, newspapers, musical compositions, songs, and works of art. Do not capitalize short conjunctions and prepositions unless they come at the beginning or the end of the title.

Desire Under the Elms   *Terminator*

Last of the Mohicans   *Of Mice and Men*

"Blueberry Hill"

6. Capitalize any title preceding a name or used as a substitute for a name. Do not capitalize a title following a name.

Judge Stone   Alfred Stone, a judge

General Clark   Raymond Clark, a general

Professor Fuentes   Harry Jones, the former president

※ Text Credits

John Batchelor, "Food, Service Hit and Miss at Gianno's," *Greensboro News & Record*, January 12, 2006. Reprinted by permission.

S. Feshbach and B. Weiner, "Pity, Anger, and Achievement Performance," from *Personality*, 1991, p. 505. Reprinted with permission of Houghton Mifflin Company.

Francis Flaherty, "The Ghetto Made Me Do It," from *In These Times*, April 5, 1993. Article is reprinted with the permission of *In These Times*, www.inthesetimes.com.

Preston Gralla, "Fast, Sleek and Shiny: Using the Internet to Help Buy New Cars," from *The Complete Idiot's Guide to Online Shopping*, by Preston Gralla, copyright © 1999 by Alpha Books. Used by permission of Alpha Books, an imprint of Penguin Group (USA).

Christopher Grant, "Graffiti: Taking a Closer Look," *The FBI Law Enforcement Bulletin*, August 1, 1996.

Adair Lara, "Who's Cheap?" from *San Francisco Chronicle*. Reprinted by permission of the author.

Janet Pearson, "Whose Values?" from *Tulsa World*, October 30, 2005. Reprinted by permission.

Ryan J. Smith, "From B'wood to the 'hood" from *Los Angeles Times*, February 19, 2006. Reprinted by permission of the author.

Gary Soto, "The Jacket" in *A Summer Life*. © 1990 by University Press of New England, Hanover, NH. Reprinted with permission.

✳ Index